CUDA Programming from Basics to Advanced

Finbarrs Oketunji

Contents

CUDA Programming from Basics to Advanced

Table of Contents

Chapter 1: Introduction to GPU and CUDA Programming

In the world of high-performance computing, Graphic Processing Units (GPUs) have emerged as powerful tools capable of performing massive parallel computations efficiently. This chapter serves as an introduction to the foundational concepts of GPU architecture and their significance in modern computing. As we explore this technology, we will focus on CUDA (Compute Unified Device Architecture), a parallel computing platform and programming model developed by NVIDIA.

CUDA allows developers to harness the power of NVIDIA GPUs by enabling them to write programs that execute on the GPU hardware with significantly enhanced performance compared to traditional CPU-only applications. The key advantage of CUDA and GPUs is their ability to manage thousands of threads concurrently, optimizing tasks that require extensive computation such as simulations, image processing, and deep learning.

We will begin by discussing the basic architecture of GPUs and how they differ from CPUs. Understanding these differences is crucial for leveraging their full potential. Following this, we will introduce the CUDA programming model, providing insights into concepts such as kernels, threads, and blocks, which are fundamental to writing efficient GPU code.

By the end of this chapter, you'll gain a solid understanding of the underpinnings of GPU architecture and CUDA programming, setting the stage for more advanced topics. Whether you are a student, researcher, or professional aiming to optimize computational tasks, this foundational knowledge is essential as you step into the world of parallel computing with CUDA.

1.1 Overview of GPU Hardware Evolution from Kepler to Hopper Architectures

The evolution of NVIDIA's GPU architectures from Kepler to Hopper marks significant milestones in parallel computing, enhancing computational throughput and introducing novel features that optimize performance for diverse applications. This progression has been pivotal for the growth of CUDA programming, enabling developers to harness enhanced capabilities for complex computations.

Kepler Architecture

Introduced in 2012, the Kepler architecture was notable for its energy efficiency and programmability improvements. It introduced the concept of Dynamic Parallelism, allowing kernels to spawn child kernels, thereby reducing the CPU's intervention during execution.

Key Features:

- Dynamic Parallelism
- GPU Boost for automatic clock speed adjustments
- Increased register file, which helps manage workloads more efficiently

Example: Here is a simple CUDA C++ example demonstrating a basic kernel launch in a Kepler-compatible way.

```cpp
#include <iostream>
#include <cuda_runtime.h>

__global__ void add(int *a, int *b, int *c, int N) {
    int idx = threadIdx.x + blockIdx.x * blockDim.x;
    if(idx < N) {
        c[idx] = a[idx] + b[idx];
    }
}

int main() {
    const int N = 256;
    int *h_a, *h_b, *h_c;
    int *d_a, *d_b, *d_c;

    // Allocate host memory
    h_a = new int[N];
    h_b = new int[N];
    h_c = new int[N];

    // Initialize host arrays
    for(int i = 0; i < N; ++i) {
        h_a[i] = i;
        h_b[i] = 2 * i;
    }

    // Allocate device memory
    cudaMalloc(&d_a, N * sizeof(int));
    cudaMalloc(&d_b, N * sizeof(int));
    cudaMalloc(&d_c, N * sizeof(int));
```

```
32    // Transfer data from host to device
33    cudaMemcpy(d_a, h_a, N * sizeof(int), cudaMemcpyHostToDevice);
34    cudaMemcpy(d_b, h_b, N * sizeof(int), cudaMemcpyHostToDevice);
35
36    // Launch the kernel
37    add<<<N/1024, 1024>>>(d_a, d_b, d_c, N);
38
39    // Transfer data from device to host
40    cudaMemcpy(h_c, d_c, N * sizeof(int), cudaMemcpyDeviceToHost);
41
42    // Free device memory
43    cudaFree(d_a);
44    cudaFree(d_b);
45    cudaFree(d_c);
46
47    // Free host memory
48    delete[] h_a;
49    delete[] h_b;
50    delete[] h_c;
51
52    return 0;
53 }
```

Maxwell and Pascal Architectures

Maxwell and Pascal further optimized the GPU design with improved performance per watt and the introduction of new memory technologies like HBM (High Bandwidth Memory).

Overview:

- Maxwell offered improved power efficiency and added NVLink support for fast interconnect.
- Pascal introduced HBM, enhancing data transfer speeds significantly.

Volta Architecture

Volta introduced the Tensor Core, a specialized unit designed to accelerate deep learning computations. It also featured unified memory enhancements and new instructions for more efficient operations.

Key Features:

- Tensor Cores for mixed-precision training
- NVSwitch for greater interconnect performance

Turing Architecture

Expanding on Volta, Turing added RT Cores for real-time ray tracing and AI-enhanced graphics. It brought significant advances to real-time image processing.

Highlights: - RT Cores for ray tracing - INT8 and INT4 precisions for AI inferencing

Ampere Architecture

Ampere doubled down on Tensor Core enhancements and introduced third-generation Tensor Cores by increasing their support for numerous data types.

Features:

- Enhanced FP32 throughput
- Third-generation Tensor Cores

Hopper Architecture

The Hopper architecture focuses on delivering advanced computational capabilities, tailored to AI and scientific workloads, setting new benchmarks for performance with multi-instance GPU capabilities and improved scalability.

Core Improvements:

- Multi-instance GPUs for concurrent workloads
- Structural sparsity features for AI

The evolution from Kepler to Hopper embodies a relentless pursuit of computational excellence, introducing features that have revolutionized the landscape of CUDA programming. As we continue to develop applications for increasingly complex tasks, understanding these hardware advancements allows us to write more efficient, scalable, and powerful CUDA programs.

Visualization of Architecture Evolution

For a visual representation of the evolution:

This diagram succinctly captures the lineage from Kepler to Hopper, each architectural shift marking a leap in GPU capabilities and CUDA possibilities. Understanding these transformations is essential for effectively employing CUDA programming techniques in cutting-edge applications.

1.2 Introduction to the CUDA 12.6 Programming Environment

The CUDA (Compute Unified Device Architecture) programming environment is a parallel computing platform and application programming interface (API) model created by NVIDIA. Its goal is to leverage the parallel computing capacity of NVIDIA GPUs for general-purpose processing. Version 12.6 introduces various enhancements and features that improve performance, usability, and compatibility with modern computing needs.

Key Features of CUDA 12.6

1. **Enhanced Performance**: CUDA 12.6 optimizes kernel launches and memory management, reducing overhead and increasing throughput.
2. **Extended Language Support**: Improved C++17 and later support, enabling more modern C++ features.
3. **Better Debugging and Profiling Tools**: Tools like Nsight Systems and Nsight Compute are more integrated, providing advanced debugging and profiling capabilities.
4. **Improved Development Workflow**: More flexible and intuitive development environment, simplifying the transition from CPU to GPU code.

Setting Up the CUDA Environment

Before diving into CUDA programming, you need to set up your development environment. Ensure you have the CUDA toolkit installed on your system. The toolkit provides essential components such as the compiler (**nvcc**), libraries, and debugging tools.

First Steps in CUDA Programming

A typical CUDA program involves writing both host (CPU) and device (GPU) code. Here's a simple C++ example illustrating the addition of two arrays using CUDA:

Host Code

The host code manages memory allocation and kernel invocation. It is written in standard C++ with CUDA-specific function calls.

```cpp
#include <iostream>
#include <cuda_runtime.h>

// Function prototypes
void checkCudaError(cudaError_t err, const char* context);
__global__ void addArrays(int* a, int* b, int* c, int size);

int main() {
    const int arraySize = 5;
    int h_a[arraySize] = {1, 2, 3, 4, 5};
    int h_b[arraySize] = {10, 20, 30, 40, 50};
    int h_c[arraySize];

    int *d_a, *d_b, *d_c;

    // Allocate device memory
    cudaError_t err = cudaMalloc((void**)&d_a, arraySize * sizeof(int));
    checkCudaError(err, "cudaMalloc - d_a");

    err = cudaMalloc((void**)&d_b, arraySize * sizeof(int));
    checkCudaError(err, "cudaMalloc - d_b");

    err = cudaMalloc((void**)&d_c, arraySize * sizeof(int));
    checkCudaError(err, "cudaMalloc - d_c");

    // Copy data from host to device
    err = cudaMemcpy(d_a, h_a, arraySize * sizeof(int),
        cudaMemcpyHostToDevice);
    checkCudaError(err, "cudaMemcpy - h_a to d_a");

    err = cudaMemcpy(d_b, h_b, arraySize * sizeof(int),
        cudaMemcpyHostToDevice);
    checkCudaError(err, "cudaMemcpy - h_b to d_b");

    // Execute kernel on the device
    addArrays<<<1, arraySize>>>(d_a, d_b, d_c, arraySize);

    // Copy result from device to host
    err = cudaMemcpy(h_c, d_c, arraySize * sizeof(int),
        cudaMemcpyDeviceToHost);
    checkCudaError(err, "cudaMemcpy - d_c to h_c");

    // Display results
    std::cout << "Result: ";
```

```
42    for (int i = 0; i < arraySize; ++i) {
43        std::cout << h_c[i] << " ";
44    }
45    std::cout << std::endl;
46
47    // Free device memory
48    cudaFree(d_a);
49    cudaFree(d_b);
50    cudaFree(d_c);
51
52    return 0;
53 }
54
55 void checkCudaError(cudaError_t err, const char* context) {
56    if (err != cudaSuccess) {
57        std::cerr << "CUDA error: " << cudaGetErrorString(err) << " in " <<
               context << std::endl;
58        exit(EXIT_FAILURE);
59    }
60 }
```

Device Code

The kernel is a function that runs on the GPU, handling parallel work.

```
1 __global__ void addArrays(int* a, int* b, int* c, int size) {
2    int idx = threadIdx.x;
3    if (idx < size) {
4        c[idx] = a[idx] + b[idx];
5    }
6 }
```

Explanation

- **Memory Management**: The host allocates both host and device memory and transfers data between them.
- **Kernel Launch**: The `addArrays` kernel is executed on the GPU with a specified configuration (`<<<1, arraySize>>>`), indicating one block with `arraySize` threads.
- **Error Handling**: The `checkCudaError` function simplifies error detection and reporting, promoting the DRY principle.

Visualization

The following diagram illustrates the memory and execution flow in a CUDA program.

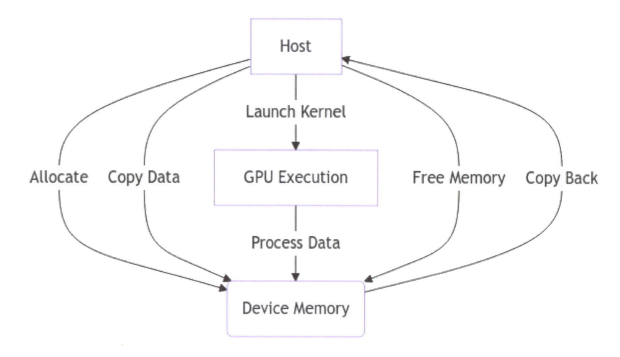

Understanding these foundational concepts is critical for effective CUDA programming. As you continue, exploring more advanced topics will open up new possibilities in parallel computing.

1.3 Enhancements in Parallel Computing for High-Performance Tasks

Parallel computing has revolutionized the way high-performance tasks are executed, particularly in fields requiring massive computational power like scientific simulations, data analysis, and machine learning. With the advent of GPUs (Graphics Processing Units) and CUDA (Compute Unified Device Architecture), parallel computing has become more accessible, allowing developers to leverage hardware acceleration for various applications.

Key Concepts in Parallel Computing with CUDA

CUDA is a parallel computing platform and application programming interface (API) model created by NVIDIA. It allows developers to use GPUs for general-purpose processing, a practice known as GPGPU (General-Purpose computing on Graphics Processing Units). Here's a brief overview of how CUDA enhances parallel computing:

1. **Massive Parallelism**: CUDA enables the execution of thousands of threads simultaneously, exploiting the GPU's architecture designed for parallel workloads.

2. **Simplified Memory Management**: CUDA provides mechanisms for managing memory effectively, including shared memory, constant memory, and global memory, optimizing data access patterns for high throughput.

3. **Streamlined Development**: With CUDA, developers can write parallel code using familiar languages like C++ while benefiting from NVIDIA's extensive libraries and tools.

C++ Code Example: Vector Addition

Below is a simple C++ CUDA example to perform vector addition, a fundamental operation in parallel computing. The task is to add two vectors and store the result in a third vector. This example adheres to best coding practices such as modularity and clarity.

```cpp
#include <iostream>
#include <cuda_runtime.h>

// Define the vector size
const int VECTOR_SIZE = 1024;

// Kernel function for vector addition
__global__ void vectorAdd(const int* A, const int* B, int* C, int size) {
    int i = blockDim.x * blockIdx.x + threadIdx.x;
    if (i < size) {
        C[i] = A[i] + B[i];
    }
}

// Utility function to check CUDA errors
void checkCudaError(cudaError_t err, const char* msg) {
    if (err != cudaSuccess) {
        std::cerr << "CUDA Error: " << msg << " - " << cudaGetErrorString(
            err) << std::endl;
        exit(EXIT_FAILURE);
    }
}

int main() {
    // Allocate host memory
    int h_A[VECTOR_SIZE], h_B[VECTOR_SIZE], h_C[VECTOR_SIZE];

    // Initialize vectors
    for (int i = 0; i < VECTOR_SIZE; ++i) {
        h_A[i] = i;
        h_B[i] = i * 2;
    }

    // Allocate device memory
    int *d_A, *d_B, *d_C;
    checkCudaError(cudaMalloc((void**)&d_A, VECTOR_SIZE * sizeof(int)), "
        Allocating d_A");
    checkCudaError(cudaMalloc((void**)&d_B, VECTOR_SIZE * sizeof(int)), "
        Allocating d_B");
    checkCudaError(cudaMalloc((void**)&d_C, VECTOR_SIZE * sizeof(int)), "
        Allocating d_C");

    // Copy data from host to device
    checkCudaError(cudaMemcpy(d_A, h_A, VECTOR_SIZE * sizeof(int),
        cudaMemcpyHostToDevice), "Copying h_A to d_A");
    checkCudaError(cudaMemcpy(d_B, h_B, VECTOR_SIZE * sizeof(int),
        cudaMemcpyHostToDevice), "Copying h_B to d_B");

    // Define block and grid sizes
    int blockSize = 256;
    int gridSize = (VECTOR_SIZE + blockSize - 1) / blockSize;

    // Launch the vector addition kernel
    vectorAdd<<<gridSize, blockSize>>>(d_A, d_B, d_C, VECTOR_SIZE);
    checkCudaError(cudaGetLastError(), "Launching vectorAdd kernel");

    // Copy the result back to host
```

```
52    checkCudaError(cudaMemcpy(h_C, d_C, VECTOR_SIZE * sizeof(int),
          cudaMemcpyDeviceToHost), "Copying d_C to h_C");
53
54    // Free device memory
55    cudaFree(d_A);
56    cudaFree(d_B);
57    cudaFree(d_C);
58
59    // Verify results
60    for (int i = 0; i < VECTOR_SIZE; ++i) {
61        if (h_C[i] != h_A[i] + h_B[i]) {
62            std::cerr << "Verification failed at index " << i << std::endl;
63            return EXIT_FAILURE;
64        }
65    }
66
67    std::cout << "Vector addition successful!" << std::endl;
68    return EXIT_SUCCESS;
69 }
```

Understanding the Example

1. **Kernel Definition**: The `vectorAdd` function is a CUDA kernel that performs the addition of two vectors. It operates on each element independently, utilizing the parallel execution model of CUDA.

2. **Error Handling**: The `checkCudaError` function ensures that any CUDA call is verified for success, thus maintaining robust error handling.

3. **Memory Management**: Efficient use of memory is illustrated by careful allocation and deallocation of device memory (`cudaMalloc` and `cudaFree`).

4. **Grid and Block Sizing**: Properly configured grid and block sizes ensure optimal performance and utilization of the GPU resources.

Visualization

For a visual representation of the vector addition process, consider the following diagram illustrating the data flow and kernel execution:

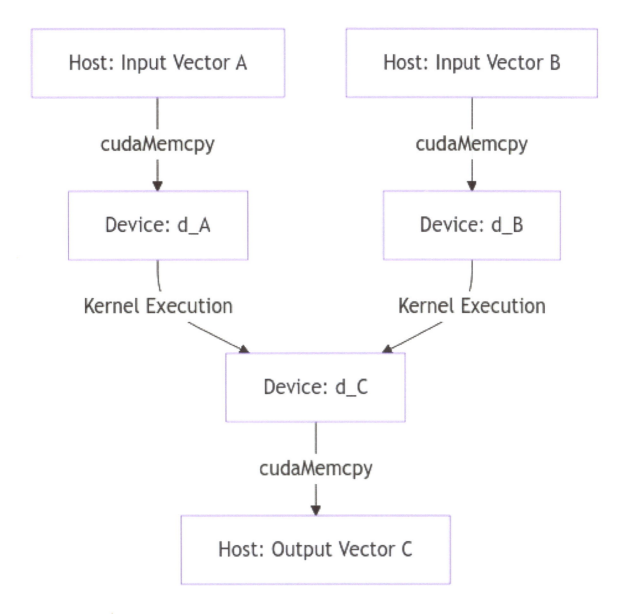

This diagram provides a high-level overview of the data transfer and processing using CUDA. By utilizing GPUs for parallel computing tasks such as vector addition, performance can be significantly improved, enabling efficient and rapid computation for high-performance tasks.

Chapter 2: Setting Up and Running CUDA 12.6

In this chapter, we will guide you through the process of setting up your development environment for CUDA 12.6. Setting up CUDA involves several steps, including installing the necessary software and configuring your system to recognize and utilize the power of NVIDIA GPUs. This foundation is crucial for developing high-performance parallel applications.

We will begin with a detailed overview of the hardware and software requirements. Understanding these prerequisites ensures that your system is fully compatible and capable of executing CUDA applications efficiently. Next, we will provide step-by-step instructions for installing CUDA 12.6, addressing common pitfalls and troubleshooting tips to avoid potential installation issues.

Once the installation process is complete, we will walk you through the process of verifying the installation. This involves running a sample CUDA program to ensure that your setup is functional and ready for development. By the end of this chapter, you will have a fully operational CUDA development environment, setting the stage for diving into CUDA programming and exploring its capabilities for optimizing computational workloads.

2.1 Step-by-step Guide to Installing CUDA 12.6 on Different Platforms

CUDA (Compute Unified Device Architecture) is essential for developing parallel applications that leverage the power of NVIDIA GPUs. Here, we will walk through installing CUDA 12.6 on different platforms: Windows, Linux, and macOS.

Installing CUDA 12.6 on Windows

1. **Verify System Requirements**:
   - Ensure you have a compatible NVIDIA GPU.
   - Check for Windows 10 or later.
2. **Download CUDA Toolkit**:
   - Visit the NVIDIA CUDA Toolkit Download Page.
   - Select the appropriate version for Windows.
3. **Install CUDA**:
   - Execute the installer.
   - Opt for 'Express' installation for beginners, or 'Custom' if you need specific components.
4. **Set Environment Variables**:
   - Go to 'System Properties' > 'Environment Variables'.
   - Append `C:\Program Files\NVIDIA GPU Computing Toolkit\CUDA\v12.6\bin` to the 'Path' variable.
5. **Verify Installation**:
   - Open Command Prompt.
   - Run `nvcc --version` to check CUDA version.
6. **Test with Sample Code**:
   - Create a simple CUDA program:

```cpp
#include <iostream>
__global__ void helloCUDA() {
    printf("Hello from CUDA Kernel!\n");
}

int main() {
    helloCUDA<<<1, 1>>>();
    cudaDeviceSynchronize();
    return 0;
}
```

   - Compile and run using `nvcc`:

```
nvcc -o helloCUDA helloCUDA.cu
helloCUDA
```

Installing CUDA 12.6 on Linux

1. **Prepare System**:
   - Update the package list: `sudo apt-get update`.
   - Install necessary dependencies: `sudo apt-get install build-essential`.
2. **Download CUDA Toolkit**:

  - Navigate to the NVIDIA CUDA Toolkit Downloads page.
  - Select the Linux distribution you're using.
3. **Install CUDA**:
  - Follow the runfile or package manager installation guide provided on the website.
  - For a runfile, change directory to the downloaded file and execute:

```
sudo sh cuda_12.6.run
```

4. **Set Environment Variables**:
  - Append the following to .bashrc:

```
export PATH=/usr/local/cuda-12.6/bin${PATH:+:${PATH}}
export LD_LIBRARY_PATH=/usr/local/cuda-12.6/lib64${
    LD_LIBRARY_PATH:+:${LD_LIBRARY_PATH}}
```

  - Source the file: source ~/.bashrc.
5. **Verify and Test**:
  - Confirm installation with nvcc --version.
  - Test with a simple program as shown in the Windows section.

Note for macOS Users

NVIDIA CUDA is not natively supported on macOS due to differences in architecture and driver's support. For developers needing CUDA on macOS, consider using a Linux virtual machine or dual-booting to Linux.

Code Visualization

To visually represent the steps involved in setting up CUDA, a flowchart can be very useful. Below is a simple diagram representing the installation process:

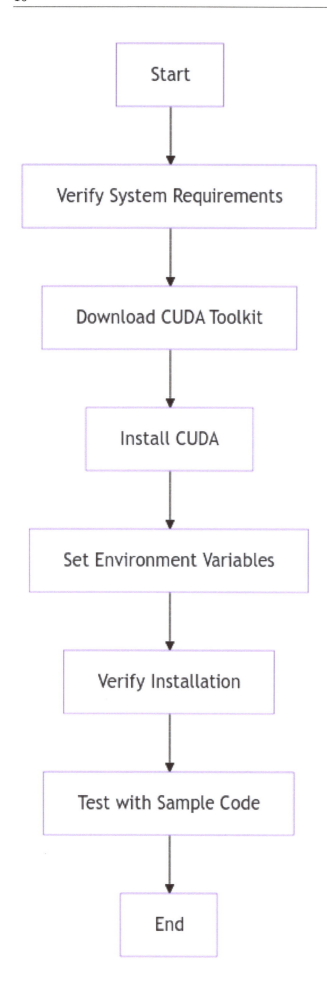

With these instructions, you should be set up to begin programming CUDA applications with efficiency and ease. Always refer to official documentation for the latest updates and troubleshoot any version-specific concerns.

2.2 Using the new NVML and Nsight Developer Tools for Monitoring and Debugging GPU Utilization

To effectively utilize NVIDIA GPUs within CUDA applications, one must monitor GPU usage and debug efficiently. NVIDIA offers the NVIDIA Management Library (NVML) and Nsight Developer Tools to facilitate these tasks. NVML provides a programmatic interface for querying GPU status and managing GPU settings, while Nsight tools assist in profiling and debugging.

NVIDIA Management Library (NVML)

NVML is a C-based API that provides comprehensive monitoring functionalities. Below is a simple example illustrating how to use NVML to query the GPU's current utilization.

C++ Example: Monitoring GPU Utilization with NVML

First, ensure that NVML is initialized and available:

```cpp
#include <nvml.h>
#include <iostream>

// Utility function to handle NVML errors
void handleNVMLReturn(nvmlReturn_t result) {
    if (result != NVML_SUCCESS) {
        std::cerr << "NVML Error: " << nvmlErrorString(result) << std::endl
            ;
        exit(EXIT_FAILURE);
    }
}

int main() {
    nvmlReturn_t result;

    // Initialize the NVML library
    result = nvmlInit();
    handleNVMLReturn(result);

    // Get the handle for the first GPU
    nvmlDevice_t device;
    result = nvmlDeviceGetHandleByIndex(0, &device);
    handleNVMLReturn(result);

    // Query the GPU utilization
    nvmlUtilization_t utilization;
    result = nvmlDeviceGetUtilizationRates(device, &utilization);
    handleNVMLReturn(result);

    // Print the utilization rates
    std::cout << "GPU Utilization: " << utilization.gpu << "%" << std::endl
        ;
    std::cout << "Memory Utilization: " << utilization.memory << "%" << std
        ::endl;
```

```
33    // Shutdown NVML
34    result = nvmlShutdown();
35    handleNVMLReturn(result);
36
37    return 0;
38 }
```

Key Points:

- **Initialization and Shutdown**: Always initialize NVML before using it and clean up with `nvmlShutdown()` after operations.
- **Error Handling**: Implement robust error handling to manage NVML's potential error states. Use helper functions like `handleNVMLReturn`.

Nsight Developer Tools

Nsight Developer Tools offers advanced capabilities to profile, debug, and trace applications. It provides in-depth visualizations of your application's performance and behavior on the GPU.

Using Nsight Systems for Profiling

Nsight Systems helps in gathering detailed performance data:

1. **Launch Nsight Systems**: Use the GUI or command line to start capturing profiling data.
2. **Set Up Profiling**: Define specific aspects like time range, processes, and system metrics you want to capture.
3. **Analyze Results**: Once captured, analyze the timeline for bottlenecks or inefficient kernel executions.

Visualizing the Concepts

Let us visualize the high-level workflow of using NVML and Nsight Systems:

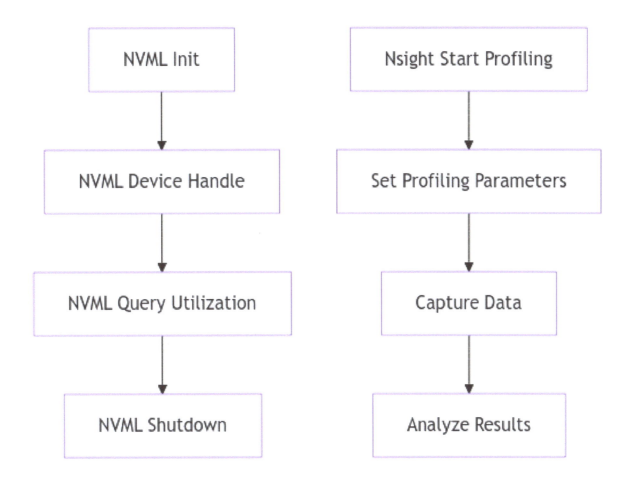

Conclusion

Using NVML and Nsight Developer Tools is crucial for managing GPU resources in CUDA applications. NVML offers a straightforward API for real-time monitoring, while Nsight's powerful profiling capabilities aid in identifying and rectifying performance bottlenecks. Integrating these tools into your workflow can ensure optimal GPU utilization and application performance.

2.3 Best Practices for Multi-Node Deployments in Large-Scale Systems

Best Practices for Multi-Node Deployments in Large-Scale Systems

Deploying multi-node systems for large-scale CUDA applications demands careful planning and execution. Below are best practices that guide setting up and running CUDA applications efficiently across multiple nodes.

1. Efficient Resource Management

Optimal Load Distribution

When deploying across nodes, it's crucial to distribute workloads effectively. Use workload profiling to understand computational demands and utilize CUDA streams and events for concurrency where feasible.

Code Example: Stream Utilization

```
#include <cuda_runtime.h>
#include <iostream>
```

```
void checkCudaError(cudaError_t err, const char* message) {
    if (err != cudaSuccess) {
        std::cerr << message << ": " << cudaGetErrorString(err) << std::
            endl;
        exit(EXIT_FAILURE);
    }
}

void performComputation(cudaStream_t stream) {
    // Placeholder for actual GPU computation
}

int main() {
    const int streamCount = 2;
    cudaStream_t streams[streamCount];

    // Create multiple CUDA streams for concurrency
    for (int i = 0; i < streamCount; ++i) {
        checkCudaError(cudaStreamCreate(&streams[i]), "Failed to create
            stream");
    }

    // Launch computations on different streams
    for (int i = 0; i < streamCount; ++i) {
        performComputation(streams[i]);
    }

    // Synchronize streams
    for (int i = 0; i < streamCount; ++i) {
        checkCudaError(cudaStreamSynchronize(streams[i]), "Stream
            synchronization failed");
        checkCudaError(cudaStreamDestroy(streams[i]), "Failed to destroy
            stream");
    }

    return 0;
}
```

2. Inter-Node Communication

Efficient Data Transfer

Utilizing high-throughput communication channels such as NVLink or RDMA (Remote Direct Memory Access) is important when transferring data between nodes. Ensure minimal data movement by processing data locally as much as possible.

Code Example: Peer-to-Peer Communication

```
#include <cuda_runtime.h>
#include <iostream>

void enablePeerAccess(int deviceCount) {
    for (int i = 0; i < deviceCount; ++i) {
        cudaSetDevice(i);
        for (int j = 0; j < deviceCount; ++j) {
            if (i != j) {
```

```
 9              cudaDeviceEnablePeerAccess(j, 0);
10          }
11      }
12   }
13 }
14
15 int main() {
16     int deviceCount;
17     cudaGetDeviceCount(&deviceCount);
18
19     if (deviceCount < 2) {
20         std::cerr << "Peer-to-peer requires at least two GPUs" << std::endl
               ;
21         return EXIT_FAILURE;
22     }
23
24     enablePeerAccess(deviceCount);
25
26     // Additional processing logic
27     return 0;
28 }
```

3. Fault Tolerance

Graceful Degradation

Implement checkpoints in the computation process to allow systems to recover from failures without needing a complete restart.

Code Example: Simple Checkpoint

```
 1 #include <fstream>
 2 #include <iostream>
 3
 4 void saveCheckpoint(const std::string& filename, int iteration) {
 5     std::ofstream checkpointFile(filename);
 6     if (checkpointFile.is_open()) {
 7         checkpointFile << "Checkpoint at iteration: " << iteration << std::
               endl;
 8         checkpointFile.close();
 9     } else {
10         std::cerr << "Unable to open checkpoint file for writing" << std::
               endl;
11     }
12 }
13
14 int main() {
15     const std::string checkpointFile = "checkpoint.txt";
16     const int checkpointInterval = 100;
17
18     for (int iteration = 0; iteration < 1000; ++iteration) {
19         // Simulated computation work
20         if (iteration % checkpointInterval == 0) {
21             saveCheckpoint(checkpointFile, iteration);
22         }
23     }
24
25     return 0;
```

```
26  }
```

4. Scalability Considerations

Adaptability

Ensure the system can scale by testing with different node and data sizes. Establish testing protocols to measure performance and bottlenecks.

5. Monitoring and Logging

Real-Time Monitoring

Implement logging mechanisms to capture performance metrics and GPU utilization in real time. This helps in identifying issues early and ensuring smooth operation.

In conclusion, successful multi-node deployments rely on efficient resource management, robust inter-node communication, and strategic fault tolerance planning. By following these best practices, you can optimize CUDA-based large-scale systems for performance and reliability.

Chapter 3: CUDA Program and Memory Hierarchy

In this chapter, we explore the foundational aspects of CUDA programming, focusing on the architecture and memory hierarchy that define its unique computational model. CUDA, developed by NVIDIA, allows for parallel programming on GPUs, offering substantial speedup over traditional CPU-based execution for specific applications.

Understanding the memory hierarchy is critical for harnessing the full potential of CUDA. This involves a clear comprehension of different memory spaces like global, shared, and local memory, each with its unique characteristics, advantages, and potential pitfalls. Recognizing how data is stored and accessed at each level enables the design of efficient and optimized CUDA programs.

We'll examine the CUDA program structure, detailing the syntax and semantics required to write effective kernels. An emphasis will be placed on memory management techniques and threading models, ensuring data is processed efficiently and correctly. By the end of this chapter, readers will grasp not just the how, but the why behind CUDA's memory strategies, setting a solid foundation for advanced topics discussed in subsequent chapters.

3.1 CUDA Program Hierarchy: Grid, Blocks, and Threads Revisited

In CUDA programming, understanding the hierarchy of grids, blocks, and threads is pivotal for writing efficient parallel code. This section revisits these concepts, providing a detailed understanding from a practical perspective, and integrates best practices in C++ with CUDA.

Conceptual Overview

CUDA leverages a three-tier hierarchy to manage parallelism:

1. **Grid**: The highest level of the hierarchy. A grid contains multiple blocks.
2. **Block**: A block is a group of threads that can cooperate among themselves. They execute the same kernel function but on different pieces of data.

3. **Thread**: The smallest unit of execution. Each thread has its own unique ID, allowing it to independently process data.

This hierarchy allows for scalable parallel execution across NVIDIA GPUs by distributing computational tasks efficiently.

Defining the Execution Configuration

An execution configuration specifies how many blocks and threads should be created when launching a kernel. Here's a straightforward example focusing on simplicity and reusability:

```cpp
#include <iostream>
#include <cuda_runtime.h>

// Kernel function to perform vector addition
__global__ void vectorAdd(const int *a, const int *b, int *c, int n) {
    int index = threadIdx.x + blockIdx.x * blockDim.x;
    if (index < n) {
        c[index] = a[index] + b[index];
    }
}

// Initializes vectors with sample data
void initializeVectors(int *a, int *b, int n) {
    for (int i = 0; i < n; ++i) {
        a[i] = i;
        b[i] = i * 2;
    }
}

int main() {
    const int arraySize = 1000;
    const int blockSize = 256; // Number of threads in each block
    const int numBlocks = (arraySize + blockSize - 1) / blockSize; // Total
        number of blocks

    // Host memory allocation
    int *h_a = new int[arraySize];
    int *h_b = new int[arraySize];
    int *h_c = new int[arraySize];

    // Initialize host vectors
    initializeVectors(h_a, h_b, arraySize);

    // Device memory allocation
    int *d_a, *d_b, *d_c;
    cudaMalloc((void**)&d_a, arraySize * sizeof(int));
    cudaMalloc((void**)&d_b, arraySize * sizeof(int));
    cudaMalloc((void**)&d_c, arraySize * sizeof(int));

    // Copy data from host to device
    cudaMemcpy(d_a, h_a, arraySize * sizeof(int), cudaMemcpyHostToDevice);
    cudaMemcpy(d_b, h_b, arraySize * sizeof(int), cudaMemcpyHostToDevice);

    // Launch the kernel - specifying grid size and block size
    vectorAdd<<<numBlocks, blockSize>>>(d_a, d_b, d_c, arraySize);

    // Copy result from device to host
```

```
47    cudaMemcpy(h_c, d_c, arraySize * sizeof(int), cudaMemcpyDeviceToHost);
48
49    // Verify and display results
50    for (int i = 0; i < 10; ++i) {
51        std::cout << "Result [" << i << "] = " << h_c[i] << std::endl;
52    }
53
54    // Free device memory
55    cudaFree(d_a);
56    cudaFree(d_b);
57    cudaFree(d_c);
58
59    // Free host memory
60    delete[] h_a;
61    delete[] h_b;
62    delete[] h_c;
63
64    return 0;
65 }
```

Best Practices

1. **Thread Management**: Ensure the number of threads handles all elements, avoiding out-of-bound access with checks like if (index < n).
2. **Modularity**: Separate initialization and data handling logic from the primary CUDA operations for clarity and reusability.
3. **Memory Management**: Always deallocate memory on both host and device to prevent leaks.

Visualization

To better understand the distribution of threads and blocks, consider the following visualization:

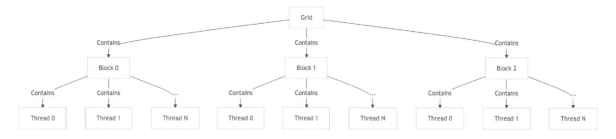

This diagram demonstrates how each grid encompasses multiple blocks, with each block managing numerous threads. Such visualization helps in understanding the parallel structure underlying CUDA programming.

3.2 New Features in CUDA Memory Management: CUB Performance Tuning and Multi-Device Scalability

CUDA continues to evolve, offering improved capabilities for managing memory efficiently, which is crucial for optimizing performance in GPU programming. Recent advancements include enhanced features for CUDA Unified Memory, the CUB (CUDA UnBounded) library for performance tuning, and improved scalability across multiple devices.

CUDA Unified Memory Enhancements

Unified Memory simplifies memory management by providing a single memory space accessible by both the CPU and GPU. Recent improvements have maximized efficiency and ease of use, enabling better overlapping of data transfer and computation.

- **Memory Prefetching**: Prefetching allows the programmer to hint at future memory access patterns, improving data locality and reducing latency. Use the `cudaMemPrefetchAsync()` function to move memory to the GPU ahead of computations.

```
// Prefetch memory to GPU
cudaMemPrefetchAsync(d_data, size, device, stream);
```

CUB Library for Performance Tuning

CUB provides a suite of high-performance primitives for CUDA, such as sorting, reduction, and prefix sum. The library has been enhanced to allow for more fine-tuned performance optimizations.

- **Efficient Memory Utilization**: Utilize CUB's memory management utilities like `CachingDeviceAllocator` to optimize memory allocation and reuse.

```
#include <cub/util_allocator.cuh>

// Create a caching allocator
cub::CachingDeviceAllocator allocator(true); // eager cleanup

// Device memory pointer
void* d_temp_storage = nullptr;
size_t temp_storage_bytes = 0;

// Initialize temporary storage
cub::DeviceReduce::Sum(d_temp_storage, temp_storage_bytes, d_in,
    d_out, num_items);
allocator.DeviceAllocate(&d_temp_storage, temp_storage_bytes);

// Execute the kernel
cub::DeviceReduce::Sum(d_temp_storage, temp_storage_bytes, d_in,
    d_out, num_items);

// Free temporary storage
allocator.DeviceFree(d_temp_storage);
```

Multi-Device Scalability

Managing multiple GPUs within a system can significantly boost performance, provided that the workload is efficiently distributed and data transfer overhead is minimized.

- **Peer-to-Peer (P2P) Memory Access**: Enable P2P memory access for faster communication between devices on the same hardware.

```
// Enable P2P access
int canAccessPeer = 0;
cudaDeviceCanAccessPeer(&canAccessPeer, device1, device2);
if (canAccessPeer) {
```

```
5        cudaDeviceEnablePeerAccess(device2, 0);
6    }
```

- **Scalable Work Distribution**: Distribute computation tasks across multiple GPUs efficiently by managing streams and dependencies. Use multi-GPU streams for concurrent kernel execution.

```
1    // Streams for each device
2    cudaStream_t streams[N];
3
4    // Initialize streams and launch kernels
5    for (int i = 0; i < N; ++i) {
6        cudaSetDevice(i);
7        cudaStreamCreate(&streams[i]);
8        myKernel<<<grid, block, 0, streams[i]>>>(deviceData[i]);
9    }
```

Best Practices

1. **Optimal Memory Access**: Always coalesce memory access to minimize latency. Use proper alignment, and favor sequential memory access patterns.
2. **Efficient Data Transfer**: Overlap data transfers with computations using streams and the asynchronous memory operations.
3. **Scalable Code Design**: Design scalable solutions catering to both single and multi-device configurations.

Visualization of Multi-Device Management

Here is a visualization of multi-device management:

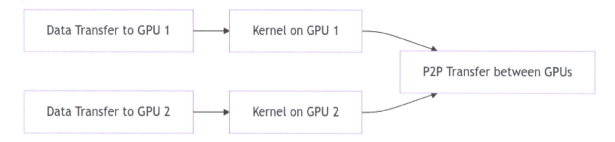

These new features in CUDA memory management facilitate more efficient and scalable GPU programming, making it easier to leverage the full capabilities of modern GPU hardware.

3.3 Improved Memory Workload Distribution Analysis with Nsight Compute 2024

When developing CUDA applications, understanding and optimizing memory workloads is crucial for achieving high performance. Nsight Compute 2024 offers enhanced tools for analyzing and improving memory workload distribution within CUDA programs.

Understanding Memory Workloads

Effective memory access patterns are key to maximizing GPU performance. Poorly distributed workloads lead to bottlenecks and inefficient use of the GPU's memory hierarchy, including global, shared, and local memory. Nsight Compute 2024 provides detailed insights into these memory access patterns, helping developers identify and rectify inefficiencies.

Utilizing Nsight Compute 2024

Nsight Compute 2024 offers a comprehensive suite of features to profile and analyze CUDA kernels. It allows developers to track memory usage and pinpoint imbalanced workloads. These features include:

- **Memory Size Metrics**: Identify excessive memory usage across kernels.
- **Access Pattern Analysis**: Evaluate how efficiently memory accesses are coalesced.
- **Per-Thread and Per-Warp Analysis**: Diagnose divergences in workload distribution.

Code Example: Optimizing Memory Access

Below is a simplified example demonstrating how to optimize memory access in a CUDA application using best practices:

```
#include <iostream>
#include <cuda_runtime.h>

#define N 1024
#define BLOCK_SIZE 256 // Choose a block size based on empirical testing

__global__ void vectorAdd(const float* A, const float* B, float* C, int
    size) {
    int idx = blockDim.x * blockIdx.x + threadIdx.x;
    if (idx < size) {
        C[idx] = A[idx] + B[idx];
    }
}

void checkCudaError(cudaError_t err, const char* msg) {
    if (err != cudaSuccess) {
        std::cerr << "Error: " << msg << ": " << cudaGetErrorString(err) <<
            std::endl;
        exit(EXIT_FAILURE);
    }
}

int main() {
    size_t size = N * sizeof(float);
    float *h_A, *h_B, *h_C; // Host pointers
    float *d_A, *d_B, *d_C; // Device pointers

    // Allocate host memory
    h_A = (float*)malloc(size);
    h_B = (float*)malloc(size);
    h_C = (float*)malloc(size);

    // Initialize vectors
    for (int i = 0; i < N; ++i) {
        h_A[i] = i;
        h_B[i] = i;
    }

    // Allocate device memory
    checkCudaError(cudaMalloc((void**)&d_A, size), "Malloc A");
```

```
39    checkCudaError(cudaMalloc((void**)&d_B, size), "Malloc B");
40    checkCudaError(cudaMalloc((void**)&d_C, size), "Malloc C");
41
42    // Copy data to device
43    checkCudaError(cudaMemcpy(d_A, h_A, size, cudaMemcpyHostToDevice), "
          Memcpy A");
44    checkCudaError(cudaMemcpy(d_B, h_B, size, cudaMemcpyHostToDevice), "
          Memcpy B");
45
46    // Kernel launch
47    int gridSize = (N + BLOCK_SIZE - 1) / BLOCK_SIZE;
48    vectorAdd<<<gridSize, BLOCK_SIZE>>>(d_A, d_B, d_C, N);
49
50    checkCudaError(cudaPeekAtLastError(), "Kernel launch");
51
52    // Copy result back to host
53    checkCudaError(cudaMemcpy(h_C, d_C, size, cudaMemcpyDeviceToHost), "
          Memcpy C");
54
55    // Cleanup
56    free(h_A);
57    free(h_B);
58    free(h_C);
59    cudaFree(d_A);
60    cudaFree(d_B);
61    cudaFree(d_C);
62
63    return 0;
64 }
```

Key Considerations

- **Block Size and Grid Configuration**: Experiment with different block sizes to determine the optimal configuration. Utilize metrics from Nsight Compute to ensure the best memory coalescing.

- **Error Handling**: Always check for CUDA errors, as illustrated in the `checkCudaError` function, to ensure robust debugging and diagnostics.

- **Memory Coalescing**: Arrange data accesses to be as contiguous as possible, which improves memory throughput.

Visualization of Memory Access Patterns

To understand the memory access patterns, let us visualize it:

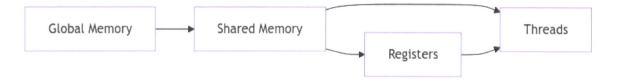

Conclusion

Nsight Compute 2024 is an invaluable tool for CUDA developers looking to refine memory workload distribution in their applications. By leveraging its insights, you can achieve optimal performance, reduce memory bottlenecks, and enhance the efficiency of your CUDA programs.

Chapter 4: Utilizing GPU-Compatible Libraries

In this chapter, we shall examine the practical application of GPU-compatible libraries to simplify and enhance CUDA programming. As the computational demands of applications grow, leveraging libraries designed for GPU acceleration becomes essential. These libraries provide pre-optimized routines that significantly reduce development time and improve performance, by providing reusable components for common tasks.

We'll explore several prominent CUDA libraries, such as cuBLAS for efficient linear algebra computations, cuFFT for fast Fourier transforms, and Thrust for high-level abstractions of data parallel algorithms. By understanding how to effectively integrate these libraries into your projects, you can harness the full power of GPUs without reinventing the wheel.

In addition to examining the functionalities of these libraries, the chapter provides practical examples to illustrate their application. You will learn how modular design and the DRY principle can be applied to CUDA programming to achieve elegant, maintainable, and high-performance code. Whether you're handling matrix operations, signal processing, or parallel algorithm implementations, mastering these libraries is a key step toward advanced CUDA programming.

4.1 Updated Libraries for GPU Computation: cuBLAS, cuFFT, and Others

In modern computing, leveraging GPU for computation-intensive tasks has become a necessity. NVIDIA provides a suite of GPU-optimized libraries that offer simple, efficient, and scalable routines for various mathematical computations. Among these libraries, cuBLAS and cuFFT are pivotal for linear algebra and Fast Fourier Transform (FFT) operations, respectively.

cuBLAS: CUDA Basic Linear Algebra Subprograms

cuBLAS provides GPU-accelerated implementations of standard BLAS (Basic Linear Algebra Subprograms) functions. These functions are essential for performance-critical linear algebra operations. The library supports operations such as vector addition, matrix multiplication, and solving linear systems.

Example: Matrix Multiplication Using cuBLAS

Here's how you can perform matrix multiplication (C = A x B) using cuBLAS:

```
#include <iostream>
#include <cublas_v2.h>
#include <cuda_runtime.h>

// Function to check CUDA errors
void checkCudaError(cudaError_t err, const char* msg) {
    if (err != cudaSuccess) {
        std::cerr << "CUDA Error: " << msg << " - " << cudaGetErrorString(
            err) << std::endl;
        exit(EXIT_FAILURE);
    }
}
```

```cpp
// Function to check cuBLAS errors
void checkCublasError(cublasStatus_t stat, const char* msg) {
    if (stat != CUBLAS_STATUS_SUCCESS) {
        std::cerr << "cuBLAS Error: " << msg << std::endl;
        exit(EXIT_FAILURE);
    }
}

// Kernel function to initialize matrices
void initializeMatrix(float* mat, int rows, int cols, float value) {
    for (int i = 0; i < rows * cols; ++i) {
        mat[i] = value;
    }
}

int main() {
    const int M = 2; // Rows in A and C
    const int N = 3; // Cols in B and C
    const int K = 3; // Cols in A, Rows in B

    float h_A[M * K], h_B[K * N], h_C[M * N];

    initializeMatrix(h_A, M, K, 1.0f); // Initialize A with 1.0
    initializeMatrix(h_B, K, N, 2.0f); // Initialize B with 2.0

    float *d_A, *d_B, *d_C;

    checkCudaError(cudaMalloc(&d_A, M * K * sizeof(float)), "Allocating A")
        ;
    checkCudaError(cudaMalloc(&d_B, K * N * sizeof(float)), "Allocating B")
        ;
    checkCudaError(cudaMalloc(&d_C, M * N * sizeof(float)), "Allocating C")
        ;

    checkCudaError(cudaMemcpy(d_A, h_A, M * K * sizeof(float),
        cudaMemcpyHostToDevice), "Copying A to device");
    checkCudaError(cudaMemcpy(d_B, h_B, K * N * sizeof(float),
        cudaMemcpyHostToDevice), "Copying B to device");

    cublasHandle_t handle;
    checkCublasError(cublasCreate(&handle), "Creating cuBLAS handle");

    const float alpha = 1.0f;
    const float beta = 0.0f;

    // Perform matrix multiplication: C = alpha * A * B + beta * C
    checkCublasError(cublasSgemm(handle, CUBLAS_OP_N, CUBLAS_OP_N, M, N, K,
        &alpha, d_A, M, d_B, K, &beta, d_C, M), "Performing SGEMM");

    checkCudaError(cudaMemcpy(h_C, d_C, M * N * sizeof(float),
        cudaMemcpyDeviceToHost), "Copying C to host");

    // Output result
    std::cout << "Result matrix C:\n";
    for (int i = 0; i < M * N; ++i) {
        std::cout << h_C[i] << " ";
        if ((i + 1) % N == 0) std::cout << '\n';
    }
```

```
64
65     // Clean up resources
66     cudaFree(d_A);
67     cudaFree(d_B);
68     cudaFree(d_C);
69     cublasDestroy(handle);
70
71     return 0;
72 }
```

This example demonstrates basic matrix multiplication using cuBLAS, showing how to manage device memory and handle errors effectively. By using modular functions, we ensure code clarity and maintainability.

cuFFT: CUDA Fast Fourier Transform

cuFFT is designed for high performance on NVIDIA GPUs and provides batch transforms for 1D, 2D, and 3D data types. FFT is widely used in scientific computing for spectral analysis, image processing, and signal processing.

Example: 1D FFT Using cuFFT

Below is an example of performing a simple 1D FFT using cuFFT:

```cpp
1  #include <iostream>
2  #include <cufft.h>
3
4  // Check cuFFT errors
5  void checkCufftError(cufftResult result, const char* msg) {
6      if (result != CUFFT_SUCCESS) {
7          std::cerr << "cuFFT Error: " << msg << std::endl;
8          exit(EXIT_FAILURE);
9      }
10 }
11
12 int main() {
13     const int N = 16; // Number of data points
14
15     cufftComplex h_data[N], h_result[N];
16     for (int i = 0; i < N; ++i) {
17         h_data[i].x = static_cast<float>(i);
18         h_data[i].y = 0.0f;
19     }
20
21     cufftComplex* d_data;
22     cudaMalloc(&d_data, sizeof(cufftComplex) * N);
23     cudaMemcpy(d_data, h_data, sizeof(cufftComplex) * N,
           cudaMemcpyHostToDevice);
24
25     cufftHandle plan;
26     checkCufftError(cufftPlan1d(&plan, N, CUFFT_C2C, 1), "Creating plan");
27     checkCufftError(cufftExecC2C(plan, d_data, d_data, CUFFT_FORWARD), "
           Executing FFT");
28
29     cudaMemcpy(h_result, d_data, sizeof(cufftComplex) * N,
           cudaMemcpyDeviceToHost);
30
```

```
31    // Output FFT result
32    std::cout << "1D FFT result:\n";
33    for (int i = 0; i < N; ++i) {
34        std::cout << "(" << h_result[i].x << ", " << h_result[i].y << ")\n"
             ;
35    }
36
37    cufftDestroy(plan);
38    cudaFree(d_data);
39
40    return 0;
41 }
```

In this example, we're performing a straightforward 1D FFT using cuFFT. Keeping the code modular and reusing error-checking functions ensures that our implementation is clean and easy to understand.

Other GPU Libraries

NVIDIA's suite of GPU libraries extends beyond cuBLAS and cuFFT. Libraries such as cuDNN for deep learning, cuSPARSE for sparse matrix operations, and cuRAND for random number generation further enhance GPU computation capabilities. Each of these libraries offers specialized functions catering to specific domains, ensuring efficient and optimized usage of GPU resources.

In summary, utilizing these GPU-compatible libraries allows developers to achieve significant performance gains with minimal code changes, following best practices for writing clean, efficient, and modular code. Keep these libraries in your toolkit to handle complex computational tasks with ease.

4.2 Leveraging the New CUB Library Updates for Performance Enhancements in CUDA 12.6

The CUB library is a collection of parallel algorithm primitives and utility functions specifically designed for CUDA. The new updates in CUB for CUDA 12.6 introduce enhancements that bolster performance and usability, making it an indispensable asset for developers aiming to optimize GPU computations. This section will examine how these updates can be leveraged effectively.

Overview of CUB Enhancements

The latest CUB update includes improvements in algorithm efficiency, support for new CUDA features, and better integration with Thrust. The library provides high-performance primitives for tasks like sorting, reduction, and scanning, which are critical for many parallel computing workflows.

Best Practices with CUB

To utilize the full potential of CUB, consider these best practices:

1. **Understand Your Data and Operations**: Choose the right CUB primitives based on the nature of your data and the operations you intend to perform.

2. **Modular Code Design**: Encapsulate CUB operations within well-defined functions to

promote reusability and maintainability.

3. **Resource Management**: Carefully manage GPU resources in your CUB operations to prevent bottlenecks and ensure efficient memory usage.

Code Example: Efficient Reduction with CUB

Let's demonstrate how to perform efficient reduction with the CUB library using CUDA 12.6. This example will highlight clean and modular code design:

```cpp
#include <cub/cub.cuh>
#include <iostream>
#include <vector>

__global__ void setupData(float* d_data, size_t size) {
    int tid = blockIdx.x * blockDim.x + threadIdx.x;
    if (tid < size) {
        d_data[tid] = tid + 1.0f; // Initialize with some data
    }
}

// Function for performing reduction using CUB
void performReduction(const std::vector<float>& h_data) {
    size_t size = h_data.size();
    float* d_data = nullptr;
    float* d_output = nullptr;
    cudaMalloc(&d_data, size * sizeof(float));
    cudaMalloc(&d_output, sizeof(float));

    cudaMemcpy(d_data, h_data.data(), size * sizeof(float),
        cudaMemcpyHostToDevice);

    void* d_temp_storage = nullptr;
    size_t temp_storage_bytes = 0;

    // Calculate the size of the temporary storage needed
    cub::DeviceReduce::Sum(d_temp_storage, temp_storage_bytes, d_data,
        d_output, size);
    cudaMalloc(&d_temp_storage, temp_storage_bytes);

    // Perform reduction
    cub::DeviceReduce::Sum(d_temp_storage, temp_storage_bytes, d_data,
        d_output, size);

    float h_output;
    cudaMemcpy(&h_output, d_output, sizeof(float), cudaMemcpyDeviceToHost);

    std::cout << "Sum: " << h_output << std::endl;

    // Clean up
    cudaFree(d_data);
    cudaFree(d_output);
    cudaFree(d_temp_storage);
}

int main() {
    const size_t size = 1024;
    std::vector<float> h_data(size);
```

```
46
47    // Setup data on GPU
48    float* d_data;
49    cudaMalloc(&d_data, size * sizeof(float));
50    setupData<<<(size + 255) / 256, 256>>>(d_data, size);
51    cudaMemcpy(h_data.data(), d_data, size * sizeof(float),
          cudaMemcpyDeviceToHost);
52    cudaFree(d_data);
53
54    // Perform reduction using CUB
55    performReduction(h_data);
56
57    return 0;
58 }
```

Explanation

- **Modular Functions**: The `performReduction` function encapsulates the reduction operation, making the code clean and reusable.
- **Efficient Memory Management**: CUDA memory is allocated and freed appropriately to avoid leaks and ensure efficiency.
- **Parallel Setup**: The `setupData` kernel is used to initialize data on the GPU, demonstrating parallel data setup.

Visualization

Below is a simple visualization of the reduction process with CUB:

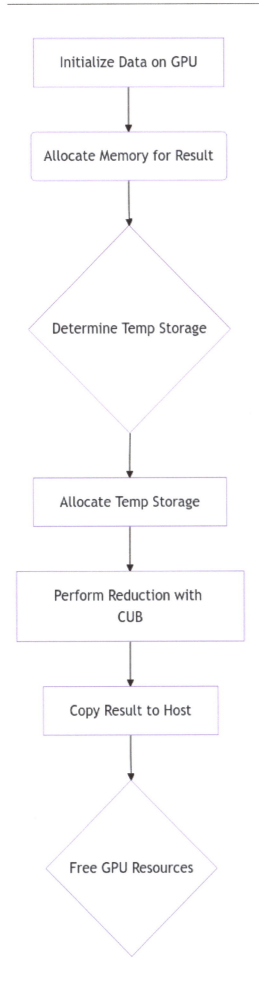

Conclusion

By adhering to best practices and leveraging the new CUB updates in CUDA 12.6, developers can achieve significant performance improvements in their GPU applications. The combination of a modular code base and efficient GPU resource management is critical for maintaining high-performance standards in complex computing tasks.

4.3 Integration with NVIDIA Collective Communications Library (NCCL) for Multi-Node Operations

NVIDIA Collective Communications Library (NCCL) is an essential tool when working with neural networks or any parallel processing tasks across multiple GPUs and nodes. NCCL provides efficient, multi-GPU communication primitives – such as broadcast, all-reduce, reduce, all-gather, and reduce-scatter – that are critical for optimizing inter-GPU communication. This section investigates integrating NCCL into your CUDA applications to leverage multi-node operations effectively.

Understanding NCCL's Role

NCCL is designed to simplify data transfers between multiple GPUs, even across different nodes, by optimizing bandwidth utilization and delivering high-performance operations akin to MPI (Message Passing Interface) but tailored for GPU communication. The key benefits of using NCCL include:

- **Scalability:** Seamless scalability across GPUs within a single node or across multiple nodes.
- **Performance:** Optimized communication that maximizes available bandwidth.
- **Simplicity:** Easy integration into existing CUDA applications.

Setting Up NCCL

Before you can use NCCL in your application, ensure that you have installed the NCCL library. Typically, NCCL comes bundled with the CUDA Toolkit. You can verify its presence and version using your package manager or CUDA toolkit version checks.

Integrating NCCL in C++ Code

The integration process involves several steps, beginning with initialization and ending with cleanup. Here's a skeleton code demonstrating the best practices in integrating NCCL with CUDA applications:

```cpp
#include <nccl.h>
#include <cuda_runtime.h>
#include <iostream>
#include <vector>

// Initialize the NCCL library
ncclComm_t initNCCLComm(int numDevices, int* deviceList, int rank) {
    ncclComm_t comm;
    ncclResult_t result = ncclCommInitRank(&comm, numDevices,
        NCCL_UNIQUE_ID, rank);
    if (result != ncclSuccess) {
        std::cerr << "NCCL initialization failed: " << ncclGetErrorString(
            result) << std::endl;
        exit(EXIT_FAILURE);
    }
```

```cpp
    return comm;
}

// Reduce operation using NCCL
void performReduce(float* sendData, float* recvData, size_t dataSize,
    ncclComm_t comm, cudaStream_t stream) {
    ncclResult_t result = ncclAllReduce(sendData, recvData, dataSize,
        ncclFloat, ncclSum, comm, stream);
    if (result != ncclSuccess) {
        std::cerr << "NCCL AllReduce failed: " << ncclGetErrorString(result
            ) << std::endl;
        exit(EXIT_FAILURE);
    }
}

// Clean up NCCL resources
void cleanupNCCLComm(ncclComm_t comm) {
    ncclResult_t result = ncclCommDestroy(comm);
    if (result != ncclSuccess) {
        std::cerr << "NCCL cleanup failed: " << ncclGetErrorString(result)
            << std::endl;
    }
}

int main() {
    const int numDevices = 2;
    int deviceList[numDevices] = {0, 1}; // Assuming 2 GPUs for simplicity
    int rank = 0; // Typically obtained from a higher-level distributed
        system manager

    // Initialize CUDA streams and NCCL communication
    std::vector<cudaStream_t> streams(numDevices);
    for (int i = 0; i < numDevices; ++i) {
        cudaSetDevice(deviceList[i]);
        cudaStreamCreate(&streams[i]);
    }

    ncclComm_t comm = initNCCLComm(numDevices, deviceList, rank);

    // Allocate and initialize device memory
    float *d_sendData, *d_recvData;
    size_t dataSize = 1024; // Example size
    cudaMalloc(&d_sendData, dataSize * sizeof(float));
    cudaMalloc(&d_recvData, dataSize * sizeof(float));

    // Perform NCCL AllReduce operation
    performReduce(d_sendData, d_recvData, dataSize, comm, streams[0]);

    // Clean up resources
    cleanupNCCLComm(comm);
    for (int i = 0; i < numDevices; ++i) {
        cudaStreamDestroy(streams[i]);
        cudaFree(d_sendData);
        cudaFree(d_recvData);
    }

    return 0;
}
```

Best Practices

1. **Error Handling:** Always check the return status of NCCL calls to catch errors early.
2. **Resource Management:** Ensure proper cleanup using `ncclCommDestroy` and `cudaStreamDestroy` to prevent resource leaks.
3. **Modularity:** Encapsulate NCCL operations in functions for reusability and maintainability.
4. **Scalability:** Design your code to easily increase the number of devices by parameterizing device counts and handling dynamic device management.

Visualizing NCCL Operations

To visualize the flow of NCCL operations, consider the following diagram, which represents the interaction between different components:

By using the NCCL library as demonstrated, you can significantly enhance the performance of multi-node GPU applications, making them more efficient and scalable without complicating your codebase.

Chapter 5: Tackling Computational Bottlenecks – Computer-Generated Holography

In this chapter, we dive into the intricacies of computer-generated holography (CGH) and explore how CUDA can significantly optimize this computationally intensive task. CGH involves complex calculations and data manipulations, presenting an ideal use case for CUDA's parallel processing capabilities. By distributing workloads across numerous GPU cores, we can achieve substantial performance gains, transforming CGH applications from theoretical concepts to practical, real-time solutions. We begin by examining the fundamental principles of holography and identifying typical bottlenecks encountered in serial computation. Step by step, we will demonstrate how to map these tasks to CUDA's architecture, ensuring improved efficiency and speed. This chapter provides both theoretical insights and practical implementations, guiding you through writing efficient CUDA code that addresses and alleviates computational bottlenecks in holography.

5.1 Solving High Computational Complexity Problems Using CUDA's Parallelisation Techniques

Computer-Generated Holography (CGH) often requires intensive computations due to the vast amount of data processing involved. Traditional sequential processing can lead to significant computational bottlenecks. CUDA (Compute Unified Device Architecture) provides a robust framework that leverages the power of parallel computing. By offloading computations to the GPU, developers can achieve substantial performance gains. In this section, we'll explore techniques for optimizing CGH computations using CUDA's parallelization capabilities with a focus on best practices in C++ programming.

Understanding Parallelization in CUDA

CUDA allows functions known as kernels to execute in parallel across many threads on a GPU. Each thread can handle a part of the data independently, drastically speeding up the computation process. We must first understand how to structure data and distribute it across threads efficiently.

Modular and Reusable Code Design

To adhere to the DRY and KISS principles, we should aim to write clean and modular code. This involves creating functions that can be reused across different parts of the program.

Example: Parallelizing a Simple Holographic Computation

Consider a simplified problem where we compute the intensity distribution of a holographic pattern. The task involves calculating the contribution of each point source to a grid of observation points.

```cpp
#include <iostream>
#include <cuda_runtime.h>

// Constants
const int GRID_SIZE = 1024;
const int BLOCK_SIZE = 16;

// CUDA Kernel for a simple holographic intensity calculation
__global__ void holographicKernel(float *intensity, const float *source,
    int gridSize) {
    // Calculate the unique thread index within the grid
    int idx = blockIdx.x * blockDim.x + threadIdx.x;

    if (idx < gridSize) {
        float x = source[idx];
        // Simulate computation for intensity based on some formula
        intensity[idx] = x * x + 2 * x + 1; // Example of a simple
            quadratic equation
    }
}

// Host function to launch the kernel
void computeHolographicIntensity(float *intensity, const float *source) {
    float *d_intensity, *d_source;

    // Allocate memory on the device
    cudaMalloc(&d_intensity, GRID_SIZE * sizeof(float));
    cudaMalloc(&d_source, GRID_SIZE * sizeof(float));

    // Copy data from host to device
    cudaMemcpy(d_source, source, GRID_SIZE * sizeof(float),
        cudaMemcpyHostToDevice);

    // Define grid and block dimensions
    dim3 blockDim(BLOCK_SIZE);
    dim3 gridDim((GRID_SIZE + BLOCK_SIZE - 1) / BLOCK_SIZE);

    // Launch the kernel
    holographicKernel<<<gridDim, blockDim>>>(d_intensity, d_source,
        GRID_SIZE);
```

```
37
38      // Copy result back to host
39      cudaMemcpy(intensity, d_intensity, GRID_SIZE * sizeof(float),
            cudaMemcpyDeviceToHost);
40
41      // Free device memory
42      cudaFree(d_intensity);
43      cudaFree(d_source);
44  }
45
46  int main() {
47      float intensity[GRID_SIZE];
48      float source[GRID_SIZE];
49
50      // Initialize the source data
51      for (int i = 0; i < GRID_SIZE; ++i) {
52          source[i] = static_cast<float>(i);
53      }
54
55      // Compute holographic intensity
56      computeHolographicIntensity(intensity, source);
57
58      // Output some results for verification
59      for (int i = 0; i < 10; ++i) {
60          std::cout << "Intensity[" << i << "] = " << intensity[i] << std::
                endl;
61      }
62
63      return 0;
64  }
```

Best Practices

- **Memory Management:** Allocate and free device memory wisely. Improper handling could lead to memory leaks and degraded performance.

- **Optimal Thread Utilization:** The block and grid dimensions should be chosen based on the problem size and GPU architecture to maximize thread utilization.

- **Kernel Design:** Keep kernels simple and focused on a specific task to enhance readability and reusability.

Visualizing Execution

For a better understanding of the execution model in CUDA, visualize the division of work among threads and blocks using a flowchart:

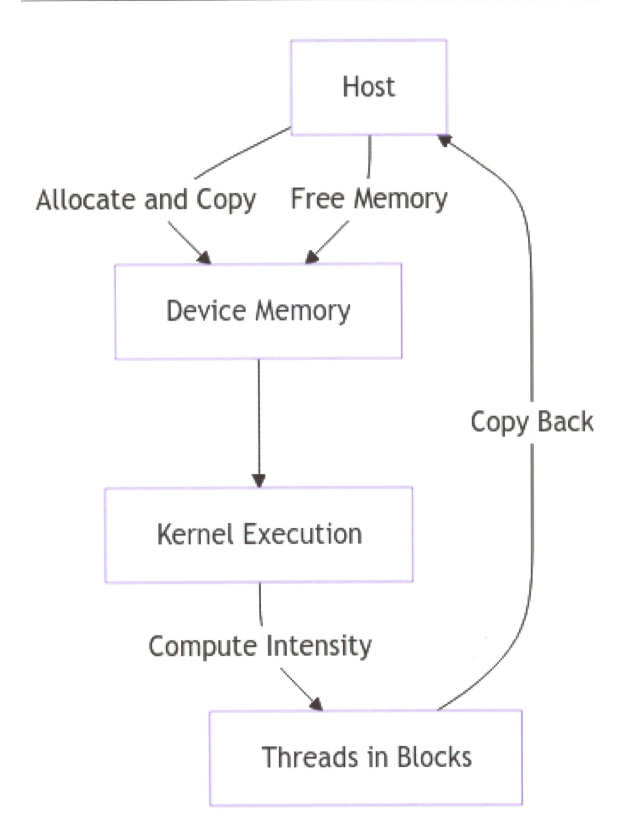

This flowchart represents the data flow and interaction between host and device memory during the execution of a CUDA program. Such a visualization helps in understanding the life cycle of data in GPU computations.

By effectively using CUDA to parallelize CGH computations, we can substantially reduce runtime and tackle the challenges posed by high computational complexity, enabling real-time holographic applications.

5.2 Performance Tuning for Memory-Heavy Operations: Leveraging Dynamic Parallelism in CUDA 12.6

When dealing with computer-generated holography, the volume of data and the complexity of computations often lead to substantial memory usage. Efficient memory management and optimal use of GPU resources are critical for ensuring performance. Here, dynamic parallelism introduced in CUDA 12.6 provides a powerful tool to optimize memory-heavy operations. This technique allows a kernel to spawn new kernels, enabling more flexible and efficient handling of complex computations directly on the GPU.

Understanding Dynamic Parallelism

Dynamic parallelism allows a kernel to launch other kernels without returning control to the host, effectively improving performance by reducing memory transfer overhead and exploiting parallel execution opportunities. This feature is particularly beneficial in scenarios where tasks are not easily predictable or require conditional execution.

Best Practices in Dynamic Parallelism

1. **Avoid Unnecessary Kernel Launches:** Limit kernel launches within a kernel. Each launch has an overhead, so ensure it is justified by the computational workload.

2. **Optimize Data Access Patterns:** Strive to achieve coalesced memory access patterns to maximize memory throughput. Ensure that threads within a warp access memory in a sequential manner.

3. **Leverage Shared Memory:** Utilize shared memory to reduce global memory accesses whenever possible. This approach significantly reduces latency.

4. **Optimize Thread Configuration:** Carefully configure grid and block dimensions to ensure maximum occupancy and efficient hardware utilization.

Example: Dynamic Kernel Launch for Holography

In holography, consider a scenario where we need to compute wavefront propagation for a complex scene. Using dynamic parallelism, we can recursively process smaller parts of the scene.

```cpp
#include <cuda_runtime.h>
#include <iostream>

// Kernel to perform complex computation
__global__ void computeWavefront(float* data, int size, int depth) {
    int idx = blockIdx.x * blockDim.x + threadIdx.x;

    if (idx >= size) return;

    // Perform a part of the computation
    data[idx] += sinf(data[idx]);

    // Recursive launch if depth allows
    if (depth > 1) {
        computeWavefront<<<1, 128>>>(data, size / 2, depth - 1);
        cudaDeviceSynchronize(); // Ensure completion of sub-kernel
    }
}
```

```
19
20  // Host function to initialize data and launch kernel
21  void launchWavefrontComputation(float* hostData, int size) {
22      float* deviceData;
23      cudaMalloc(&deviceData, size * sizeof(float));
24      cudaMemcpy(deviceData, hostData, size * sizeof(float),
               cudaMemcpyHostToDevice);
25
26      computeWavefront<<<(size + 127) / 128, 128>>>(deviceData, size, 3);
27      cudaMemcpy(hostData, deviceData, size * sizeof(float),
               cudaMemcpyDeviceToHost);
28
29      cudaFree(deviceData);
30  }
31
32  int main() {
33      const int dataSize = 1024;
34      float* data = new float[dataSize];
35
36      // Initialize data
37      for (int i = 0; i < dataSize; ++i) {
38          data[i] = static_cast<float>(i);
39      }
40
41      launchWavefrontComputation(data, dataSize);
42
43      // Output results
44      for (int i = 0; i < 10; ++i) {
45          std::cout << data[i] << " ";
46      }
47      std::cout << std::endl;
48
49      delete[] data;
50      return 0;
51  }
```

Visualization

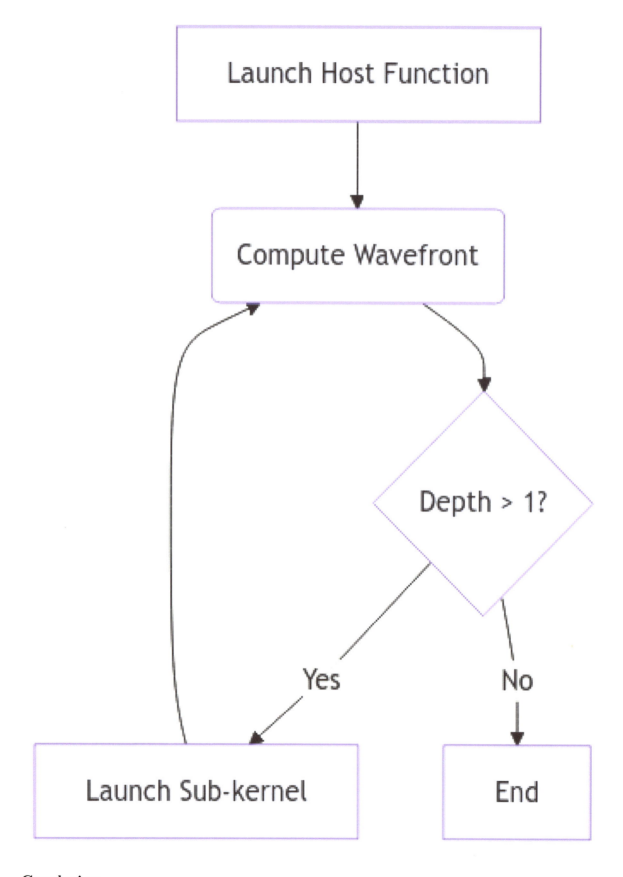

Conclusion

Leveraging dynamic parallelism in CUDA 12.6 for memory-heavy operations enables handling complex and recursive problems efficiently on the GPU. By structuring code to minimize kernel launches and optimize memory usage, we can significantly reduce computational bottle-necks in computer-generated holography, ultimately enhancing performance and scalability. Remember, effective use of dynamic parallelism is rooted in careful planning and understanding of both your algorithm and CUDA architecture.

Chapter 6: Conditional Branching in Simulations – Monte Carlo Method for Optical Properties

In this chapter, we explore the use of conditional branching for simulating complex systems using CUDA, focusing on the Monte Carlo Method for modeling optical properties. The Monte Carlo method is a powerful stochastic technique employed to solve problems that are deterministic in principle but complex in practice. Applications range from modeling light transport in tissues for medical imaging to complex photon scattering in materials.

We begin by introducing the basic principles of the Monte Carlo method, emphasizing its applicability in simulating the interaction of light with varying materials. Conditional branching plays a pivotal role here, as we need to decide the fate of photons based on probabilistic models, often leading to divergent paths within the simulation.

Understanding how to efficiently implement these conditional branches in CUDA is crucial for leveraging the full potential of GPU parallelism. The chapter progresses from simple to more sophisticated examples, demonstrating how to minimize warp divergence—a common issue where different threads in a warp take different execution paths—which can significantly impact performance.

By structuring our CUDA code to handle conditional branching effectively, we can create scalable and high-performance simulations. The chapter concludes with practical examples and coding exercises to reinforce the concepts learned, providing a solid foundation for building more advanced Monte Carlo simulations in CUDA.

6.1 Optimizing Branching in CUDA Code Using Warp-Level Programming

In CUDA programming, optimizing conditional branching is crucial for maximizing performance, particularly in simulations like the Monte Carlo method for optical properties. Conditional branches can lead to warp divergence, where threads in a warp follow different execution paths, causing serialization and reducing parallel efficiency. Efficient management of conditional branches is achievable through warp-level programming techniques, which leverage the architecture of CUDA-enabled GPUs.

Understanding Warp Divergence

A warp is a group of 32 threads that execute the same instruction. When threads within a warp encounter a conditional branch, they may diverge, causing some to wait while others execute different code paths. This can significantly degrade performance, especially in computations that heavily rely on branching, such as Monte Carlo simulations.

Warp-Level Intrinsics for Optimizing Branching

CUDA provides intrinsics that operate at the warp level, allowing threads to communicate efficiently and make decisions collectively. Key intrinsics include `__ballot_sync()`, `__any_sync()`, and `__all_sync()`, which can be used to evaluate conditions across the threads in a warp efficiently. Let's explore how to use these intrinsics to optimize branching.

Example: Using `__ballot_sync()` for Warp-Level Branching

Suppose we need to determine if any thread in a warp needs to execute a particular code block. Instead of letting each thread evaluate the condition independently, we can use `__ballot_sync()` to gather information about the condition across the warp.

```cpp
#include <cuda_runtime.h>
#include <iostream>

// Kernel function to demonstrate warp-level branching optimization
__global__ void monteCarloSimulation(float* results, const int numTrials) {
    int tid = blockIdx.x * blockDim.x + threadIdx.x;
    int lane_id = threadIdx.x % 32; // Lane ID within a warp

    // Arbitrary condition for demonstration
    bool condition = (tid % 2 == 0);

    // Use __ballot_sync to check the condition across the warp
    unsigned int mask = __ballot_sync(0xFFFFFFFF, condition);

    if (condition) {
        // If any thread in the warp meets the condition, execute this
            block
        if (lane_id == 0) {
            // Perform computation just once per warp
            // ... your computation logic here
            results[tid / 32] = 42.0f; // Sample result
        }
    }

    // Ensure all threads in the warp are synchronized
    __syncwarp();
}

int main() {
    const int numTrials = 1024;
    float* d_results;
    cudaMalloc(&d_results, numTrials / 32 * sizeof(float));

    // Launch the kernel
    monteCarloSimulation<<<numTrials / 256, 256>>>(d_results, numTrials);

    // Cleanup
    cudaFree(d_results);

    return 0;
}
```

Explanation

1. **Determine the Lane ID**: Each thread calculates its lane ID within its warp using `threadIdx.x % 32`.

2. **Evaluate Condition Collectively**: The condition is evaluated for all threads in the warp using `__ballot_sync()`, which returns a mask representing the evaluation result for all threads.

3. **Execute Conditional Code**: If the condition is met for any thread in the warp, the computation is performed once per warp by a designated thread (e.g., `lane_id == 0`).

4. **Synchronization**: Ensure warp-level synchronization with `__syncwarp()` to maintain correct data flow across threads.

Visualizing Warp-Level Execution

Here's a simple visualization of how warp-level branching works:

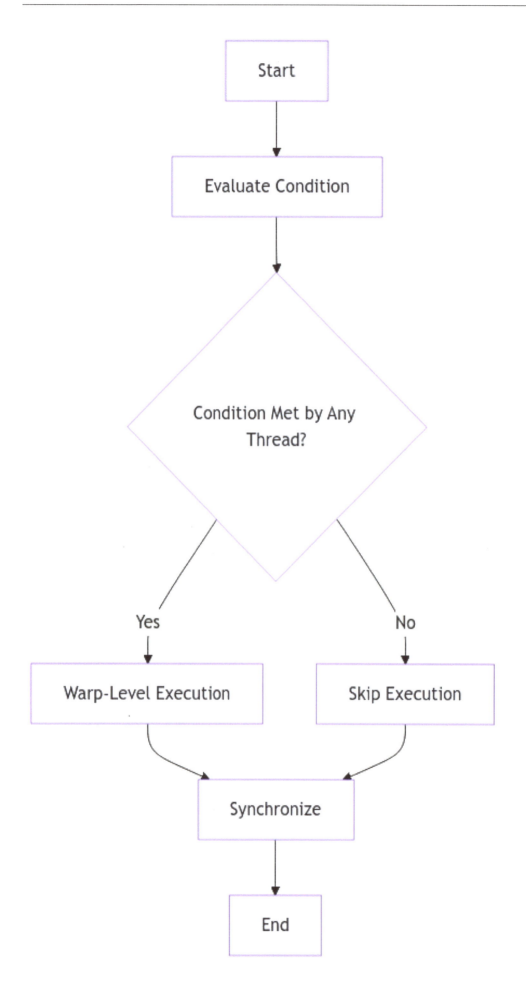

Conclusion

By optimizing branching using warp-level programming, Monte Carlo simulations for optical properties can achieve improved performance. Utilizing warp-level intrinsics minimizes warp divergence, making code execution more efficient and faster. Embrace these best practices to enhance your CUDA applications, ensuring they run smoothly even with complex conditional logic.

6.2 Enhancements to Monte Carlo Simulations for Optical Properties with Improved Random Number Generation Techniques in CUDA 12.6

Monte Carlo simulations are a fundamental tool in computational optics, often used to model the interaction of light with complex materials. A crucial aspect of these simulations is the random number generation, which must be both efficient and accurate, particularly when implemented in a CUDA environment. In CUDA 12.6, new techniques have been introduced to enhance random number generation, providing improvements in speed and statistical quality.

Improved Random Number Generation in CUDA 12.6

CUDA 12.6 introduces the cuRAND library, which facilitates high-performance, high-quality random number generation. This library is optimized for running on NVIDIA GPUs and offers a wide array of distributions and generators. Using cuRAND, we can ensure that our Monte Carlo simulations not only execute faster but also yield more reliable results.

Key Features of cuRAND in CUDA 12.6

1. **Performance Optimization:** The generators are optimized for parallel execution, maximizing throughput.
2. **Statistical Quality:** Provides random numbers that pass rigorous statistical tests.
3. **Ease of Use:** Designed to be straightforward to incorporate into existing CUDA applications.

Implementing Random Number Generation with cuRAND

Below is a modular C++/CUDA example demonstrating how to set up and use the cuRAND library for generating random numbers in a Monte Carlo simulation:

```cpp
#include <curand_kernel.h>
#include <iostream>

// Define constants for the simulation
constexpr int NUM_THREADS = 256;
constexpr int NUM_BLOCKS = 32;

// Kernel for initializing the random states
__global__ void initRandomStates(curandState *state, unsigned long seed) {
    int id = threadIdx.x + blockIdx.x * blockDim.x;
    curand_init(seed, id, 0, &state[id]); // Initialize with a seed,
        sequence number, and offset
}

// Kernel for performing Monte Carlo simulation
__global__ void monteCarloSimulation(curandState *state, float *results) {
    int id = threadIdx.x + blockIdx.x * blockDim.x;
    curandState localState = state[id];
```

```
19    // Simulate optical properties using random numbers
20    float randomValue = curand_uniform(&localState);
21
22    // A simple operation representing the simulation logic
23    results[id] = randomValue * randomValue;  // Replace with actual
          optical property computation
24
25    // Save the updated state back
26    state[id] = localState;
27 }
28
29 int main() {
30    // Allocate memory for random states and results
31    curandState *devStates;
32    cudaMalloc(&devStates, NUM_THREADS * NUM_BLOCKS * sizeof(curandState));
33
34    float *results;
35    cudaMalloc(&results, NUM_THREADS * NUM_BLOCKS * sizeof(float));
36
37    // Initialize random states
38    initRandomStates<<<NUM_BLOCKS, NUM_THREADS>>>(devStates, time(NULL));
39
40    // Run the Monte Carlo simulation
41    monteCarloSimulation<<<NUM_BLOCKS, NUM_THREADS>>>(devStates, results);
42
43    // Transfer the results back to the host (not shown here for simplicity
          )
44    // Free allocated memory
45    cudaFree(devStates);
46    cudaFree(results);
47
48    return 0;
49 }
```

Explanation and Best Practices

- **Initialization:** We initialize random states using `initRandomStates()`, setting up each thread with a unique state. This step is critical for avoiding correlations between parallel threads.

- **Simulation Kernel:** The `monteCarloSimulation()` kernel performs the actual computation, generating and using random numbers to simulate optical properties. Note how each thread operates independently, ensuring parallel scalability.

- **Memory Management:** Properly allocate and free device memory using `cudaMalloc()` and `cudaFree()`, respectively, to manage resources efficiently.

- **Scalability:** By adjusting the number of blocks and threads, the simulation can be scaled to match the computational capacity of the GPU.

Visualizing Monte Carlo Execution Flow

For a better understanding of the Monte Carlo workflow in a CUDA environment, consider the following diagram:

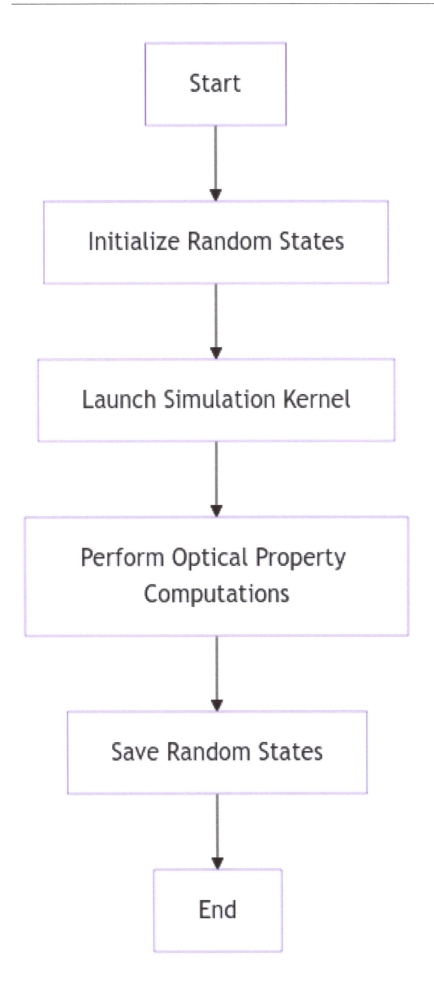

Using these techniques, you can leverage CUDA 12.6's capabilities to create highly efficient and accurate Monte Carlo simulations for optical properties. This approach not only enhances the performance but also ensures the statistical robustness of your simulations, making it well-suited for advanced optical modeling.

Chapter 7: Overcoming Memory Access Bottlenecks – Electromagnetic Field Simulation Using FDTD Method

Chapter 7 examines the intricacies of optimizing memory access patterns, a critical factor when leveraging GPU architectures for computationally intensive tasks. Specifically, this chapter focuses on implementing the Finite-Difference Time-Domain (FDTD) method to simulate electromagnetic fields within CUDA. FDTD is a widely used computational technique, but its performance can be hindered by memory access inefficiencies. By understanding how to manage memory on a GPU strategically, you can significantly enhance the performance of your FDTD simulations.

This chapter will guide you through the nuances of memory hierarchy in CUDA, emphasizing the importance of coalesced memory access, and the minimization of global memory usage while maximizing shared memory. We will explore optimizing data locality and discuss the trade-offs involved in different memory allocation strategies. Through clear examples and detailed explanations, you will learn how to adapt FDTD algorithms to leverage CUDA's architecture effectively, ultimately reducing computational bottlenecks and improving simulation efficiency.

7.1 Best Practices for Optimising Memory Access with the CUDA Graph API

When optimizing memory access for an Electromagnetic Field Simulation using the Finite-Difference Time-Domain (FDTD) method, leveraging the CUDA Graph API can be profoundly beneficial. It provides a mechanism to optimize the task graph of your application, reducing overheads associated with kernel launches and enhancing memory access patterns. The following are best practices to achieve optimal performance:

1. Use Unified Memory with Prefetching

Unified Memory simplifies data management between CPU and GPU, and when combined with prefetching, it can significantly optimize data access times. Prefetching data to the GPU can reduce latency.

```
#include <cuda_runtime.h>

// Allocate memory using Unified Memory and prefetch it to the GPU
void allocateAndPrefetch(float** data, size_t size) {
    cudaMallocManaged(data, size * sizeof(float));
    cudaMemPrefetchAsync(*data, size * sizeof(float), 0, cudaStreamDefault)
        ;
}
```

2. Implement CUDA Graph API for Task Management

CUDA Graphs allow you to define task dependencies and improve the concurrency of your simulation kernels. This reduces the overhead of kernel launches significantly.

```
#include <cuda_runtime.h>
#include <iostream>

```

```
4  // A simple kernel for updating the electromagnetic field
5  __global__ void updateFieldKernel(float* field, size_t size) {
6      int idx = blockIdx.x * blockDim.x + threadIdx.x;
7      if (idx < size) {
8          field[idx] += 1.0f; // Simple operation for demonstration
9      }
10 }
11
12 void runSimulationGraph(float* field, size_t size) {
13     cudaGraph_t graph;
14     cudaGraphExec_t graphExec;
15
16     cudaStreamBeginCapture(cudaStreamDefault, cudaStreamCaptureModeGlobal);
17     updateFieldKernel<<<(size + 255) / 256, 256>>>(field, size);
18     cudaStreamEndCapture(cudaStreamDefault, &graph);
19
20     cudaGraphInstantiate(&graphExec, graph, nullptr, nullptr, 0);
21     cudaGraphLaunch(graphExec, cudaStreamDefault);
22     cudaStreamSynchronize(cudaStreamDefault);
23
24     // Clean up
25     cudaGraphDestroy(graph);
26     cudaGraphExecDestroy(graphExec);
27 }
```

3. Optimize Memory Access Patterns

Coalesce memory accesses to ensure that global memory reads and writes are efficient. This means aligning your data structures and access patterns to match GPU memory architecture.

```
1  // Ensure coalesced memory access by accessing data in a linear fashion
2  __global__ void coalescedAccessKernel(float* data, size_t width, size_t
     height) {
3      int x = blockIdx.x * blockDim.x + threadIdx.x;
4      int y = blockIdx.y * blockDim.y + threadIdx.y;
5
6      if (x < width && y < height) {
7          size_t index = y * width + x; // Ensure alignment and coalescing
8          data[index] *= 2.0f; // Example operation
9      }
10 }
```

4. Leverage Asynchronous Memory Transfers

Utilize asynchronous memory operations to overlap computation with data transfers, thus reducing idle times.

```
1  void asyncMemoryCopy(float* hostData, float* deviceData, size_t size) {
2      cudaMemcpyAsync(deviceData, hostData, size * sizeof(float),
         cudaMemcpyHostToDevice, cudaStreamDefault);
3      // Launch kernel or other operations while memory copy is in progress
4  }
```

Visualization

The following is a visualization of a CUDA Graph leveraging dependencies and stream management:

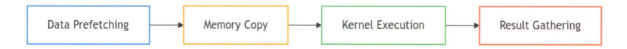

Conclusion

By following these best practices for optimizing memory access using the CUDA Graph API, you can significantly improve the performance of your electromagnetic field simulations. Efficient memory management, combined with the task orchestration capabilities of CUDA Graphs, reduces access bottlenecks and enhances overall throughput.

7.2 Exploiting New Memory Access Patterns in Unified Memory to Accelerate FDTD Simulations

In electromagnetic field simulations using the Finite-Difference Time-Domain (FDTD) method, memory access patterns play a critical role in determining the performance efficiency. Traditionally, explicit memory management using `cudaMalloc` and `cudaMemcpy` has been employed to transfer data between host and device memory. However, the advent of Unified Memory in CUDA allows for more flexible and efficient memory management, particularly beneficial in applications like FDTD simulations where data dependencies can lead to complex memory access patterns.

Understanding Unified Memory

Unified Memory simplifies memory management by providing a single memory space accessible by both the CPU and the GPU. This allows for on-demand data migration, simplifying data access patterns and reducing the overhead of explicit data transfers. Unified Memory is particularly useful in FDTD simulations, where data grids are frequently updated and accessed by both host and device.

Enhancing FDTD with New Memory Access Patterns

In FDTD simulations, the key to acceleration lies in optimizing the memory access to minimize latency and maximize throughput. By exploiting Unified Memory, we can define new access patterns that allow kernels to access data directly in a manner that reduces cache misses and improves spatial locality.

Implementation Example

Consider a simple 1D FDTD simulation for electromagnetic waves. We will demonstrate how to define a kernel and use Unified Memory for efficient memory access. Below is a modular and reusable C++ example:

```cpp
#include <iostream>
#include <cuda_runtime.h>

// Define the number of grid points
const int GRID_SIZE = 1024;
const int TIME_STEPS = 500;

// CUDA error checking
#define CUDA_CHECK(err) {\
    if (err != cudaSuccess) {\
        std::cerr << "CUDA error: " << cudaGetErrorString(err) << " at line
            " << __LINE__ << std::endl;\
```

```
12        exit(EXIT_FAILURE);\
13    }\
14 }
15
16 // Kernel for updating electric and magnetic fields
17 __global__ void updateFields(float* eField, float* hField, int gridSize) {
18     int idx = blockIdx.x * blockDim.x + threadIdx.x;
19     if (idx < gridSize - 1) {
20         eField[idx] += 0.1f * (hField[idx] - hField[idx - 1]);
21     }
22     if (idx < gridSize) {
23         hField[idx] += 0.1f * (eField[idx + 1] - eField[idx]);
24     }
25 }
26
27 // Main function
28 int main() {
29     float *eField, *hField;
30
31     // Allocate Unified Memory
32     CUDA_CHECK(cudaMallocManaged(&eField, GRID_SIZE * sizeof(float)));
33     CUDA_CHECK(cudaMallocManaged(&hField, GRID_SIZE * sizeof(float)));
34
35     // Initialize fields
36     for (int i = 0; i < GRID_SIZE; ++i) {
37         eField[i] = 0.0f;
38         hField[i] = 0.0f;
39     }
40
41     // Define block and grid sizes
42     int blockSize = 256;
43     int gridSize = (GRID_SIZE + blockSize - 1) / blockSize;
44
45     // Time-stepping loop
46     for (int t = 0; t < TIME_STEPS; ++t) {
47         updateFields<<<gridSize, blockSize>>>(eField, hField, GRID_SIZE);
48         CUDA_CHECK(cudaDeviceSynchronize());
49     }
50
51     // Free Unified Memory
52     CUDA_CHECK(cudaFree(eField));
53     CUDA_CHECK(cudaFree(hField));
54
55     std::cout << "Simulation completed successfully!" << std::endl;
56     return 0;
57 }
```

Advantages of This Approach

1. **Simplicity**: Unified Memory automatically handles data migration, simplifying code and reducing the scope for errors.
2. **Performance**: By avoiding explicit `cudaMemcpy` calls, we reduce overhead and allow the CUDA driver to optimize data transfers.
3. **Modularity**: Code is clean and modular, adhering to DRY and KISS principles, facilitating easy updates and maintenance.

Visualizing Memory Access Patterns

To better understand how memory access patterns work with Unified Memory, consider the following visualization:

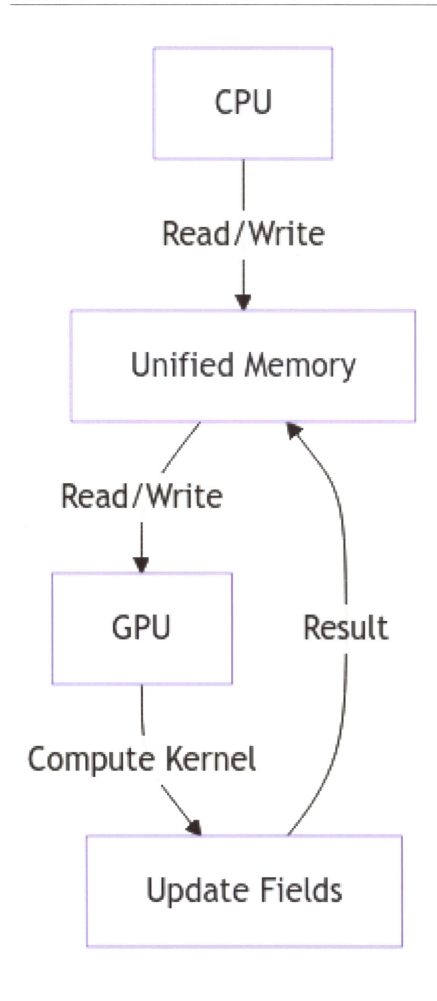

This diagram illustrates the direct access between CPU, Unified Memory, and GPU, showcasing the streamlined memory flow and simplified interactions enabled by Unified Memory.

In conclusion, leveraging new memory access patterns with Unified Memory in FDTD simulations can lead to substantial performance gains while simplifying memory management. This approach is crucial for achieving efficient and scalable solutions in electromagnetic field simulations.

Chapter 8: Chapter 8: Fortran Implementation in CUDA – Numerical Solutions to Heat Conduction

In chapter 8, we will look into integrating Fortran code within CUDA to achieve enhanced computational efficiency in solving numerical problems, specifically focusing on heat conduction. This chapter is designed to guide you through leveraging CUDA's parallel processing capabilities while utilizing Fortran's established numerical computation strengths. By addressing heat conduction, a fundamental issue in various scientific and engineering fields, this chapter provides a practical context for understanding how these two powerful computing paradigms can be combined. You'll explore the intricacies of setting up a CUDA environment for Fortran, writing efficient kernels, and optimizing data transfer between host and device. Real-world examples will illustrate how to achieve significant performance improvements, making computational tasks not only faster but also more resource-efficient.

8.1 Implementing Numerical Methods in CUDA Fortran for Solving Partial Differential Equations

The heat conduction equation, a common partial differential equation (PDE), is a fundamental example in scientific computing that describes how heat diffuses through a medium over time. Solving such equations numerically, particularly in parallel, can significantly benefit from GPU acceleration via CUDA. Though our primary focus here is on CUDA Fortran, let's first explore some essential numerical methods and demonstrate C++ snippets as a part of the computational logic which can be employed in a similar approach.

Understanding the Heat Conduction Equation

The one-dimensional heat equation can be expressed as:

```
u /t =    *  ²u /x²
```

where:

- u(x,t) is the temperature at position x and time t
-    is the thermal diffusivity constant

This equation can be discretised using finite differences, leading to the following time-stepping scheme:

```
u[i]^(n+1) = u[i]^n + ( * Δt / Δx²) * (u[i-1]^n - 2u[i]^n + u[i+1]^n)
```

In this representation:

- Partial derivatives are shown as
- Superscripts are indicated with ^
- Subscripts are shown in square brackets []

- Greek letters are spelled out (e.g.,   for alpha)
- Δ represents the delta symbol

CUDA Fortran Implementation Strategy

When implementing numerical methods to solve these equations on a GPU using CUDA Fortran, we focus on the core computational kernel, memory management, and efficient parallel execution. Here's how you can implement the explicit scheme mentioned above.

1. **Data Management**: Use device and host arrays to manage data to be processed on the GPU.
2. **Kernel Launching**: Efficiently map the computations over the grid and blocks.
3. **Memory Transfers**: Minimize memory transfer between host and device.

Code Example in C++ for Reference

Before diving into Fortran, consider this concise example in C++ for educational purposes. It prepares a simple numerical method for heat conduction:

```cpp
#include <iostream>
#include <vector>

constexpr int N = 100;       // Number of spatial points
constexpr int steps = 1000;  // Number of time steps
constexpr double alpha = 0.01;
constexpr double dt = 0.1;
constexpr double dx = 0.1;

// Function to initialize the temperature field
void initialize(std::vector<double>& u) {
    for (int i = 0; i < N; ++i) {
        u[i] = (i == N/2) ? 100.0 : 0.0;  // Initial condition: Hot in the
            middle
    }
}

// Function to perform time-stepping
void time_step(std::vector<double>& u, std::vector<double>& u_new) {
    for (int i = 1; i < N-1; ++i) {
        u_new[i] = u[i] + alpha * dt / (dx * dx) * (u[i+1] - 2 * u[i] + u[i
            -1]);
    }
}

int main() {
    std::vector<double> u(N, 0.0), u_new(N, 0.0);

    initialize(u);

    for (int step = 0; step < steps; ++step) {
        time_step(u, u_new);
        u.swap(u_new); // Swap pointers for next iteration
    }

    for (const auto& temp : u) {
        std::cout << temp << " ";
    }
```

```
37    std::cout << std::endl;
38
39    return 0;
40 }
```

Visualizing the Computational Model

To visualize the computational grid and data flow, consider the diagram below. Each block represents a spatial point, and arrows indicate the data dependencies in the numerical scheme.

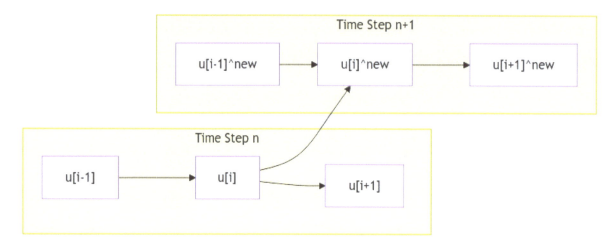

Conclusion

Crafting a CUDA Fortran implementation involves understanding the mathematical formulation, designing the computational grid, and managing memory smartly to leverage GPUs' parallel capabilities. While the snippet provided is in C++ for conceptual clarity, similar principles apply in Fortran with appropriate CUDA directives, making it straightforward to port the serial logic to a parallel GPU environment. This approach ensures modularity and adherence to DRY and KISS principles.

8.2 Enhancements in CUDA Fortran for Better Memory Management and Performance Scaling

CUDA Fortran has brought several enhancements that streamline memory management and improve performance scaling, essential for efficiently executing numerical solutions to heat conduction problems. By understanding and applying these enhancements, programmers can optimize data handling and leverage GPU capabilities effectively.

Unified Memory

Unified Memory in CUDA allows a single memory space accessible by both the CPU and GPU, reducing the intricacy of memory management. Fortran developers can benefit from this feature by simplifying memory allocation and ensuring seamless data transfer.

```
1 #include <iostream>
2
3 // A simple Unified Memory example in C++
4 __global__ void incrementKernel(int* data, int N) {
5     int idx = blockIdx.x * blockDim.x + threadIdx.x;
6     if (idx < N) {
```

```
7        data[idx]++;
8      }
9  }
10
11 int main() {
12     const int N = 100;
13     int* data;
14
15     // Unified memory allocation
16     cudaMallocManaged(&data, N * sizeof(int));
17
18     // Initialize data
19     for (int i = 0; i < N; ++i) {
20         data[i] = i;
21     }
22
23     // Launch kernel with N/256 blocks and 256 threads per block
24     incrementKernel<<<(N + 255) / 256, 256>>>(data, N);
25
26     // Wait for GPU to finish
27     cudaDeviceSynchronize();
28
29     // Clean up
30     cudaFree(data);
31
32     return 0;
33 }
```

Streamlined Memory Coalescing

Efficient memory coalescing is vital for maximizing throughput. CUDA Fortran enhancements enable better alignment and access patterns, ensuring contiguous memory accesses, which minimizes latency.

Asynchronous Memory Transfers

Utilizing asynchronous memory operations can significantly enhance performance by overlapping computation with data transfers. This allows the GPU to perform calculations while simultaneously moving data in and out of memory.

```
1  #include <iostream>
2  #include <cuda_runtime.h>
3
4  // Asynchronous memory transfer example in C++
5  void asyncTransferExample() {
6      const int N = 100;
7      float* hostData = new float[N];
8      float* deviceData;
9
10     for (int i = 0; i < N; ++i) {
11         hostData[i] = static_cast<float>(i);
12     }
13
14     // Allocate device memory
15     cudaMalloc(&deviceData, N * sizeof(float));
16
17     cudaStream_t stream;
```

```
18    cudaStreamCreate(&stream);
19
20    // Asynchronous transfer from host to device
21    cudaMemcpyAsync(deviceData, hostData, N * sizeof(float),
          cudaMemcpyHostToDevice, stream);
22
23    // Perform other tasks while transfer occurs
24    // ...
25
26    // Synchronize stream
27    cudaStreamSynchronize(stream);
28
29    // Clean up
30    cudaStreamDestroy(stream);
31    cudaFree(deviceData);
32    delete[] hostData;
33 }
```

Improved Kernel Launch Management

Optimized kernel launches with appropriate configurations are crucial for performance scaling. CUDA Fortran provides more flexible control over grid and block dimensions, aligning computation with the data structure and problem size.

Modular Functions and Clean Design

Adopting a modular approach in kernel design leads to enhanced readability and maintainability. Ensuring that functions are concise and reusable supports both DRY and KISS principles, which are essential in complex computational problems.

```
1  #include <iostream>
2
3  // Modular approach
4  __global__ void processData(int* data, int N) {
5      int idx = blockIdx.x * blockDim.x + threadIdx.x;
6      if (idx < N) {
7          data[idx] = idx * idx;  // Example operation
8      }
9  }
10
11 void launchKernel(int* data, int N) {
12     int blockSize = 256;
13     int numBlocks = (N + blockSize - 1) / blockSize;
14     processData<<<numBlocks, blockSize>>>(data, N);
15 }
16
17 int main() {
18     const int N = 1000;
19     int* data;
20
21     // Allocate memory
22     cudaMallocManaged(&data, N * sizeof(int));
23
24     // Launch kernel
25     launchKernel(data, N);
26
27     // Wait for GPU
```

```
28      cudaDeviceSynchronize();
29
30      // Deallocate memory
31      cudaFree(data);
32
33      return 0;
34 }
```

By leveraging these enhancements, CUDA Fortran developers can effectively execute heat conduction simulations while maximizing performance and memory efficiency. These practices ensure a scalable and adaptable solution tailored to the specific needs of numerical computing on GPUs.

Chapter 9: GPU Programming with OpenCL

In the ever-evolving landscape of parallel computing, harnessing the power of GPUs provides significant performance advantages for various computational tasks. While CUDA is a prevalent choice for NVIDIA GPUs, OpenCL offers a cross-platform alternative, compatible with a broader range of devices from multiple vendors. This chapter focuses on introducing OpenCL as a complementary tool for GPU programming, equipping you with the knowledge to write efficient and portable code that can run on any OpenCL-compliant device.

The chapter begins with a comprehensive overview of the OpenCL architecture, covering its platform model, memory hierarchy, and execution model. This foundation will help you understand how OpenCL abstracts the underlying hardware to provide a unified programming interface.

Next, we look into setting up an OpenCL environment and writing your first simple program. You will learn about the key components such as platforms, contexts, command queues, and kernels, and how they interrelate to enable parallel execution on a GPU.

We will then explore in detail the process of writing, compiling, and executing OpenCL kernels. Special attention is given to memory management, including efficient data transfer between host and device, and utilizing various memory types such as global, local, and private memory to optimize performance.

Additionally, advanced topics such as synchronization, event handling, and leveraging OpenCL's interoperability with other APIs are covered, providing you with the skills to tackle complex problems with high efficiency.

By the end of this chapter, you will not only understand how to program with OpenCL but also appreciate its role in the broader GPU programming ecosystem, allowing you to choose the right tool for your specific computational needs.

9.1 Introduction to OpenCL for Cross-Platform GPU Programming

OpenCL (Open Computing Language) is an open standard developed to allow programs to execute across heterogeneous platforms, combining CPUs, GPUs, and other processors. Unlike CUDA, which is specific to NVIDIA GPUs, OpenCL is designed to be cross-platform, making it a versatile choice for applications targeting various hardware.

Key Concepts of OpenCL

1. **Platform Model**: OpenCL defines a host connected to one or more OpenCL devices.

Each device consists of compute units, which in turn consist of processing elements.

2. **Execution Model**: OpenCL uses a kernel-based execution model. Kernels are functions that execute on OpenCL devices, similar to CUDA kernels.

3. **Memory Model**: OpenCL provides several memory regions:

   - Global Memory
   - Constant Memory
   - Local Memory
   - Private Memory

4. **Programming Model**: OpenCL programs are divided into host and device codes. The host code (written in C/C++/Python) manages device operations, while the device code (written in OpenCL C) executes on the compute devices.

Best Practices for OpenCL in C++

- **Modular Design**: Separation of concerns is crucial. Organize your host and kernel code efficiently to maximize readability and reusability.

- **Resource Management**: Proper management of OpenCL objects like contexts, command queues, and memory buffers is essential to prevent resource leaks.

- **Error Handling**: OpenCL API errors should be handled consistently. Use utility functions for error checks.

Simple C++ Example with OpenCL

```cpp
#include <CL/cl.hpp>
#include <iostream>
#include <vector>

// Utility function to check OpenCL errors
inline void checkError(cl_int error, const std::string &message) {
    if (error != CL_SUCCESS) {
        std::cerr << message << " Error Code: " << error << std::endl;
        exit(EXIT_FAILURE);
    }
}

// Simple Kernel to add two vectors
const char* vectorAddKernelSource = R"CLC(
    __kernel void vector_add(__global const float* a,
                             __global const float* b,
                             __global float* result) {
        int index = get_global_id(0);
        result[index] = a[index] + b[index];
    }
)CLC";

int main() {
    std::vector<float> a = {1.0f, 2.0f, 3.0f};
    std::vector<float> b = {4.0f, 5.0f, 6.0f};
    std::vector<float> result(3);

    // Step 1: Set up Platform and Device
```

```
cl::Platform platform = cl::Platform::getDefault();
cl::Device device = platform.getDevices(CL_DEVICE_TYPE_GPU).front();

// Step 2: Create Context and Command Queue
cl::Context context(device);
cl::CommandQueue queue(context, device);

// Step 3: Create Buffers
cl::Buffer bufferA(context, CL_MEM_READ_ONLY | CL_MEM_COPY_HOST_PTR, a.
    size() * sizeof(float), a.data());
cl::Buffer bufferB(context, CL_MEM_READ_ONLY | CL_MEM_COPY_HOST_PTR, b.
    size() * sizeof(float), b.data());
cl::Buffer bufferResult(context, CL_MEM_WRITE_ONLY, result.size() *
    sizeof(float));

// Step 4: Build Kernel
cl::Program program(context, vectorAddKernelSource, true);
cl::Kernel kernel(program, "vector_add");

// Step 5: Set Kernel Arguments
kernel.setArg(0, bufferA);
kernel.setArg(1, bufferB);
kernel.setArg(2, bufferResult);

// Step 6: Execute Kernel
cl::NDRange globalSize(a.size());
queue.enqueueNDRangeKernel(kernel, cl::NullRange, globalSize);
queue.finish();

// Step 7: Read Results
queue.enqueueReadBuffer(bufferResult, CL_TRUE, 0, result.size() *
    sizeof(float), result.data());

// Display Results
std::cout << "Result: ";
for (float value : result) {
    std::cout << value << " ";
}
std::cout << std::endl;

return 0;
}
```

Visualization

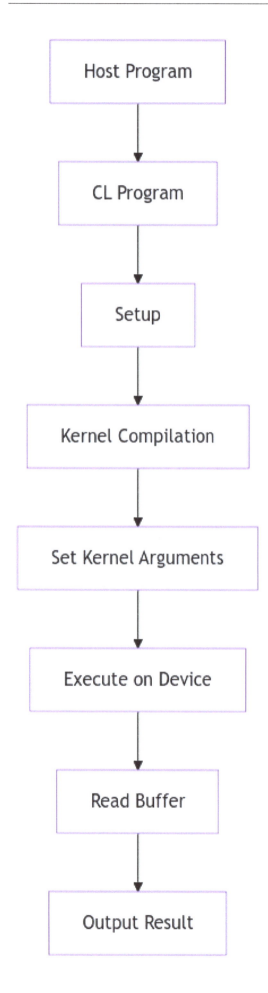

This example illustrates the OpenCL process of setting up a simple vector addition kernel, showcasing the separation of duties between host and device, as well as emphasizing clean and maintainable code practices.

9.2 Comparison of OpenCL and CUDA 12.6 in Terms of Performance and Portability

In the realm of GPU programming, both OpenCL and CUDA present compelling options. While they serve similar purposes, their design philosophies and target audiences lead to distinct strengths and weaknesses. In this section, we will focus on comparing OpenCL and CUDA 12.6 in terms of performance and portability, providing insights with clean C++ code examples.

Performance

CUDA is tightly integrated with NVIDIA hardware, allowing for extensive optimization. This results in superior performance on NVIDIA GPUs. OpenCL, meanwhile, is designed to be platform-agnostic, providing reasonable performance across a variety of hardware.

Example: Matrix Multiplication in CUDA

Let's consider a simple matrix multiplication example in CUDA, where we can take advantage of NVIDIA-specific optimizations.

```
#include <cuda_runtime.h>
#include <iostream>

#define N 256

__global__ void matrixMulCUDA(float *C, float *A, float *B, int width) {
    int tx = threadIdx.x;
    int ty = threadIdx.y;

    float pValue = 0.0;
    for (int k = 0; k < width; ++k) {
        float a = A[ty * width + k];
        float b = B[k * width + tx];
        pValue += a * b;
    }
    C[ty * width + tx] = pValue;
}

void launchKernel(float *h_C, float *h_A, float *h_B, int size) {
    float *d_A, *d_B, *d_C;
    size_t bytes = size * size * sizeof(float);

    cudaMalloc((void**)&d_A, bytes);
    cudaMalloc((void**)&d_B, bytes);
    cudaMalloc((void**)&d_C, bytes);

    cudaMemcpy(d_A, h_A, bytes, cudaMemcpyHostToDevice);
    cudaMemcpy(d_B, h_B, bytes, cudaMemcpyHostToDevice);

    dim3 threadsPerBlock(N, N);
    matrixMulCUDA<<<1, threadsPerBlock>>>(d_C, d_A, d_B, size);

    cudaMemcpy(h_C, d_C, bytes, cudaMemcpyDeviceToHost);
```

```
34
35      cudaFree(d_A);
36      cudaFree(d_B);
37      cudaFree(d_C);
38 }
39
40 int main() {
41      int size = N;
42      float h_A[N * N], h_B[N * N], h_C[N * N];
43
44      launchKernel(h_C, h_A, h_B, size);
45
46      std::cout << "Matrix multiplication completed." << std::endl;
47      return 0;
48 }
```

Performance Considerations

- **Memory Management:** CUDA provides finer control over GPU memory, allowing for optimization more tailored to specific hardware configurations.
- **Optimized Libraries:** CUDA benefits from libraries such as cuBLAS and cuDNN which provide highly optimized routines.

Portability

OpenCL's main strength lies in its portability. It is designed to run on CPUs, GPUs, and other processors from multiple vendors. This broad compatibility makes OpenCL attractive for developers targeting multiple platforms.

Example: Matrix Multiplication in OpenCL

Here's an equivalent matrix multiplication example using OpenCL:

```
1  #include <CL/cl.hpp>
2  #include <iostream>
3  #include <vector>
4
5  #define N 256
6
7  const char* kernelSource = R"(
8      __kernel void matrixMul(
9          __global float* C,
10         __global float* A,
11         __global float* B,
12         const unsigned int width)
13     {
14         int tx = get_global_id(0);
15         int ty = get_global_id(1);
16
17         float value = 0.0;
18         for (int k = 0; k < width; ++k) {
19             value += A[ty * width + k] * B[k * width + tx];
20         }
21         C[ty * width + tx] = value;
22     }
23 )";
24
```

```
25  void runOpenCLMatrixMul() {
26      std::vector<float> h_A(N * N), h_B(N * N), h_C(N * N);
27
28      cl::Context context(CL_DEVICE_TYPE_GPU);
29      cl::Program program(context, kernelSource);
30      program.build();
31
32      cl::Buffer bufferA(context, CL_MEM_READ_ONLY, N * N * sizeof(float));
33      cl::Buffer bufferB(context, CL_MEM_READ_ONLY, N * N * sizeof(float));
34      cl::Buffer bufferC(context, CL_MEM_WRITE_ONLY, N * N * sizeof(float));
35
36      cl::CommandQueue queue(context);
37      queue.enqueueWriteBuffer(bufferA, CL_TRUE, 0, N * N * sizeof(float),
            h_A.data());
38      queue.enqueueWriteBuffer(bufferB, CL_TRUE, 0, N * N * sizeof(float),
            h_B.data());
39
40      cl::Kernel kernel(program, "matrixMul");
41      kernel.setArg(0, bufferC);
42      kernel.setArg(1, bufferA);
43      kernel.setArg(2, bufferB);
44      kernel.setArg(3, N);
45
46      cl::NDRange global(N, N);
47      queue.enqueueNDRangeKernel(kernel, cl::NullRange, global);
48      queue.enqueueReadBuffer(bufferC, CL_TRUE, 0, N * N * sizeof(float), h_C
            .data());
49
50      std::cout << "Matrix multiplication completed using OpenCL." << std::
            endl;
51  }
52
53  int main() {
54      runOpenCLMatrixMul();
55      return 0;
56  }
```

Portability Considerations

- **Vendor-Neutral:** OpenCL code runs on diverse hardware, albeit sometimes with varying performance.
- **Platform Flexibility:** The same code can run across CPUs, GPUs, and other accelerators, providing a more flexible deployment environment.

Visualization

To visualize the potential execution flow and resources involved for both CUDA and OpenCL, we can use a flowchart.

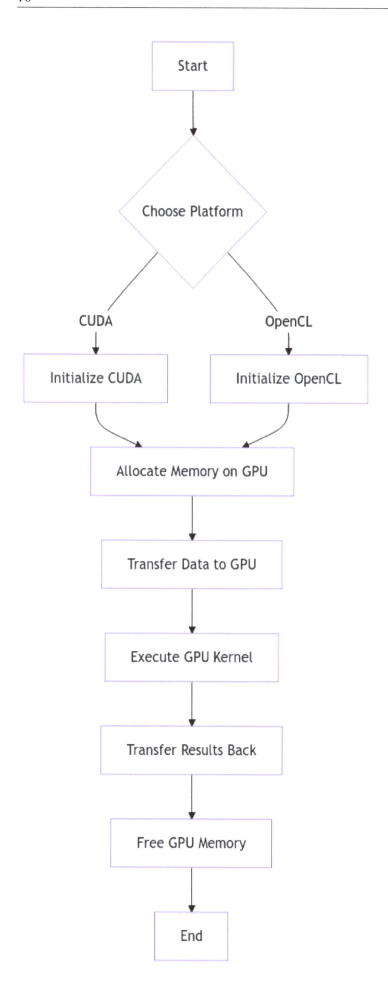

Summary

While CUDA generally offers higher performance on NVIDIA hardware due to its deep integration and bespoke optimizations, OpenCL wins on portability across diverse computing environments. The choice between them often depends on the target hardware and specific performance requirements of the application.

9.3 New Updates in OpenCL to Support NVIDIA's Latest GPU Architectures

OpenCL continues to evolve, ensuring compatibility and performance optimization for the latest NVIDIA GPU architectures. With each update, OpenCL refines its capabilities, offering developers tools to leverage the full potential of advanced hardware. This section discusses the significant updates tailored for NVIDIA's cutting-edge GPUs and provides illustrative C++ code snippets adhering to best practices.

Key Updates

1. **Enhanced Parallelism**: The latest OpenCL versions have improved support for concurrent task execution, which maximizes the utilization of NVIDIA GPUs.

2. **Memory Management Improvements**: OpenCL now offers more efficient ways to handle device memory, reducing latency and improving data throughput.

3. **Advanced Synchronization Primitives**: New synchronization features ensure better coordination between compute units, crucial for optimizing performance on multi-core environments.

4. **Improved Profiling Tools**: With enhanced profiling capabilities, developers can better analyze and fine-tune their applications for NVIDIA hardware.

C++ Code Example

The following example illustrates some of these updates, focusing on memory management and synchronization. It involves matrix multiplication, a common GPU task, and highlights modular and reusable code design.

```cpp
#include <CL/cl.hpp>
#include <iostream>
#include <vector>

// Kernel code in a string format
const char* kernelSource = R"CLC(
    __kernel void matrixMultiply(__global float* A, __global float* B,
        __global float* C, const int N) {
        int row = get_global_id(0);
        int col = get_global_id(1);
        float result = 0.0f;
        for (int k = 0; k < N; ++k) {
            result += A[row * N + k] * B[k * N + col];
        }
        C[row * N + col] = result;
    }
)CLC";

void checkError(cl_int error, const std::string& message) {
```

```cpp
    if (error != CL_SUCCESS) {
        throw std::runtime_error(message + " Error Code: " + std::to_string
            (error));
    }
}

// Initializes OpenCL and performs matrix multiplication
void performMatrixMultiplication(const std::vector<float>& A, const std::
    vector<float>& B, std::vector<float>& C, const int N) {
    cl_int err;
    cl::Platform platform = cl::Platform::get(&err);
    checkError(err, "Failed to get OpenCL platform");

    cl::Device device;
    platform.getDevices(CL_DEVICE_TYPE_GPU, &device);

    cl::Context context(device, nullptr, nullptr, nullptr, &err);
    checkError(err, "Failed to create OpenCL context");

    cl::Program program(context, kernelSource, true, &err);
    checkError(err, "Failed to build OpenCL program");

    cl::Kernel kernel(program, "matrixMultiply", &err);
    checkError(err, "Failed to create kernel");

    cl::CommandQueue queue(context, device, 0, &err);
    checkError(err, "Failed to create command queue");

    // Allocate buffer memory for matrices
    cl::Buffer bufferA(context, CL_MEM_READ_ONLY | CL_MEM_COPY_HOST_PTR,
        sizeof(float) * N * N, const_cast<float*>(A.data()), &err);
    cl::Buffer bufferB(context, CL_MEM_READ_ONLY | CL_MEM_COPY_HOST_PTR,
        sizeof(float) * N * N, const_cast<float*>(B.data()), &err);
    cl::Buffer bufferC(context, CL_MEM_WRITE_ONLY, sizeof(float) * N * N,
        nullptr, &err);

    checkError(err, "Failed to create buffers");

    // Set kernel arguments
    kernel.setArg(0, bufferA);
    kernel.setArg(1, bufferB);
    kernel.setArg(2, bufferC);
    kernel.setArg(3, N);

    // Define global and local work size
    cl::NDRange global(N, N);

    // Enqueue the kernel execution
    queue.enqueueNDRangeKernel(kernel, cl::NullRange, global, cl::NullRange
        );
    queue.finish();

    // Read results from device
    queue.enqueueReadBuffer(bufferC, CL_TRUE, 0, sizeof(float) * N * N, C.
        data());
}

int main() {
```

```
70    const int N = 1024; // Assume a 1024x1024 matrix
71    std::vector<float> A(N * N, 1.0f);
72    std::vector<float> B(N * N, 1.0f);
73    std::vector<float> C(N * N, 0.0f);
74
75    try {
76        performMatrixMultiplication(A, B, C, N);
77        std::cout << "Matrix multiplication completed successfully!" << std
              ::endl;
78    } catch (const std::runtime_error& e) {
79        std::cerr << e.what() << std::endl;
80    }
81
82    return 0;
83 }
```

Conclusion

By embracing these updates in OpenCL, developers can efficiently harness the power of NVIDIA's latest GPU architectures. This ensures optimized performance and enhanced capabilities, driving forward the possibilities in GPU programming. Keep your code modular, reusable, and clean as demonstrated to handle increasingly complex computations effectively.

Chapter 10: Using Nsight Compute 2024 for Performance Tuning

In high-performance computing, optimizing your CUDA applications to run efficiently on NVIDIA GPUs is essential. This chapter introduces Nsight Compute 2024, a powerful profiling tool designed to help developers gain insight into GPU performance and identify bottlenecks. We will begin by exploring the intuitive interface and features of Nsight Compute that enable detailed performance analysis. You will learn how to leverage these features to collect data, assess kernel execution metrics, and pinpoint areas needing attention. By the end of this chapter, you'll understand how to effectively utilize Nsight Compute to refine your CUDA code, achieving optimal performance and resource utilization.

10.1 Leveraging Nsight Compute 2024's New Features: Workload Distribution Analysis and Warp-State Tracking

In this section, we explore two powerful features of Nsight Compute 2024—workload distribution analysis and warp-state tracking—that are pivotal in optimizing CUDA applications for enhanced performance. These tools offer insights into the intricacies of GPU execution, allowing developers to identify bottlenecks and optimize resource utilization effectively.

Understanding Workload Distribution Analysis

Workload distribution analysis provides a detailed breakdown of how computational tasks are spread across GPU threads. This feature is instrumental in identifying imbalances, which might lead to inefficient utilization of GPU resources. Efficient workload distribution ensures each thread in a block is optimally utilized, minimizing idle periods and maximizing throughput.

Practical Use Case

Consider a scenario where your CUDA kernel involves manipulating a large matrix. Using workload distribution analysis, you can evaluate whether each thread in a block is performing a comparable amount of work, thereby avoiding scenarios where some threads complete their tasks much earlier than others.

Here is a simple example kernel where workload imbalance can be detected and improved:

```cpp
#include <cuda_runtime.h>
#include <iostream>

__global__ void imbalanceKernel(int *data, int size) {
    int idx = blockIdx.x * blockDim.x + threadIdx.x;

    // Simple condition causing imbalance
    if (idx < size) {
        data[idx] *= 2; // Double the value
    }
}

void checkCudaErrors(cudaError_t err) {
    if (err != cudaSuccess) {
        std::cerr << "CUDA error: " << cudaGetErrorString(err) << std::endl
            ;
        exit(1);
    }
}

int main() {
    const int arraySize = 1024;
    int *d_data;

    checkCudaErrors(cudaMalloc(&d_data, arraySize * sizeof(int)));
    checkCudaErrors(cudaMemset(d_data, 1, arraySize * sizeof(int)));

    dim3 blocks(16);
    dim3 threads(64);

    imbalanceKernel<<<blocks, threads>>>(d_data, arraySize);
    checkCudaErrors(cudaDeviceSynchronize());

    cudaFree(d_data);
    return 0;
}
```

In this kernel, workload distribution analysis can reveal that threads beyond the last valid index (size) are underutilized due to the conditional operation, indicating a need for kernel boundary adjustments or use of alternative strategies such as loop unrolling or workload sharing.

Exploring Warp-State Tracking

Warp-state tracking provides insights into the operational state of each warp during execution. This feature is essential for understanding issues like warp divergence, which can significantly degrade performance. Warp divergence occurs when threads within a warp follow different execution paths due to conditional branching, leading to serialized execution instead of parallel.

Practical Use Case

Consider a kernel where conditional logic within the loop introduces warp divergence. Warp-state tracking can help pinpoint the divergent paths and their impact on performance.

Example kernel with potential warp divergence:

```
__global__ void divergentKernel(int *data, int size) {
    int idx = blockIdx.x * blockDim.x + threadIdx.x;

    if (idx < size) {
        if (data[idx] % 2 == 0) {
            data[idx] /= 2;
        } else {
            data[idx] = (data[idx] * 3) + 1;
        }
    }
}
```

In this example, warp-state tracking would indicate divergence due to the conditional branch. To minimize divergence, consider restructuring the kernel to group similar operations, thereby improving warp efficiency.

Visualizing Execution Flow

To better understand the execution flow and potential points of optimization, visualization tools can be employed. Below is a conceptual illustration of a kernel's execution flow:

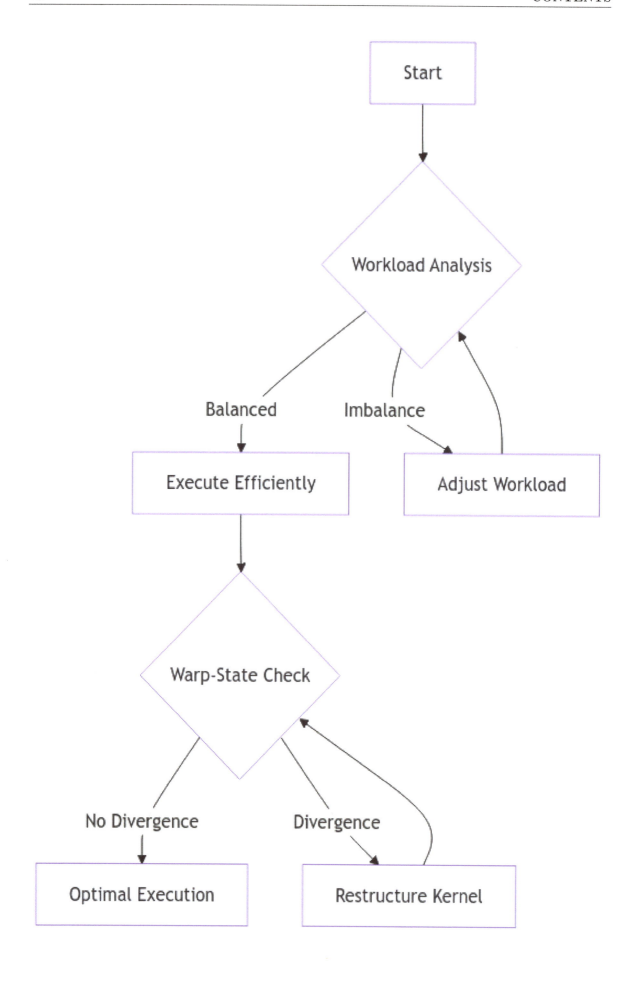

This flowchart visualizes the process of evaluating workload distribution and warp-state conditions, guiding necessary adjustments for performance enhancement.

By effectively leveraging Nsight Compute 2024's workload distribution analysis and warp-state tracking features, developers can optimize CUDA applications, ensuring they meet performance objectives while utilizing GPU resources efficiently.

10.2 How to Optimize CUDA Kernels Using Nsight Compute's Advanced Profiling Tools

Nsight Compute is an invaluable tool for profiling and optimizing CUDA kernels. By analyzing various kernel execution metrics, you can identify performance bottlenecks, improve resource utilization, and ultimately enhance application efficiency. Here's how you can optimize CUDA kernels using Nsight Compute's advanced profiling tools effectively:

Understanding Nsight Compute's Profiling Metrics

Nsight Compute provides a wide array of metrics, such as warp occupancy, memory bandwidth, and execution dependencies. Familiarity with these metrics helps pinpoint inefficiencies in your CUDA kernels. Key metrics to focus on include:

- **Occupancy**: Measures the utilization of the GPU's multiprocessors. Higher occupancy generally suggests better parallelism.
- **Memory Throughput**: Indicates the efficiency of memory operations. Aim for coalesced access patterns to improve bandwidth.
- **Instruction Replay**: High rates may indicate ineffective utilization; strive to minimize replays.

Step 1: Collect Baseline Performance Data

Begin by running Nsight Compute to gather initial performance data. Use the command line interface to collect this data:

```
nv-nsight-cu-cli --profile-from-start 0 --kernel-regex "myKernel" ./
    my_cuda_application
```

This command profiles only "myKernel," minimizing data collection to areas of interest.

Step 2: Identify Bottlenecks

Inspect the collected data using Nsight Compute's GUI or CLI tool. Look for low occupancy, memory bottlenecks, or high latency instructions. Once bottlenecks are identified, you can start implementing optimizations.

Step 3: Code Modification for Optimization

When modifying your code, adhere to best practices. For example, consider the following optimizations for memory usage and thread management:

- **Memory Coalescing**: Ensure global memory accesses are coalesced. Replace inefficient memory access patterns with coalesced ones.

```
// Before optimization: Inefficient memory access pattern
__global__ void myKernel(float *d_data) {
    int idx = threadIdx.x + blockDim.x * blockIdx.x;
```

```
 4      // Non-coalesced access
 5      float value = d_data[idx * stride];
 6      // Perform operations
 7  }
 8
 9  // After optimization: Coalesced memory access
10  __global__ void optimizedKernel(float *d_data) {
11      int idx = threadIdx.x + blockDim.x * blockIdx.x;
12      // Coalesced access
13      float value = d_data[idx];
14      // Perform operations
15  }
```

- **Thread Convergence**: Minimize divergent branching within warps to improve efficiency.

```
 1  // Before optimization: Divergent branching
 2  if (threadIdx.x % 2 == 0) {
 3      // Some operation
 4  } else {
 5      // Another operation
 6  }
 7
 8  // After optimization: Unified path for threads
 9  int condition = (threadIdx.x % 2);
10  switch (condition) {
11      case 0:
12          // Some operation
13          break;
14      case 1:
15          // Another operation
16          break;
17  }
```

Step 4: Validate Changes

After making optimizations, rerun the profiler to ensure changes lead to performance improvements. Compare the new metrics with your baseline and iteratively refine your approach.

Step 5: Use Advanced Features

Nsight Compute offers advanced features such as source code correlation, which allows you to correlate performance metrics directly with lines of code. This can be extremely helpful in identifying the exact source of bottlenecks.

Visualization

To understand the flow of kernel execution and optimization steps, visualize the process using a flowchart:

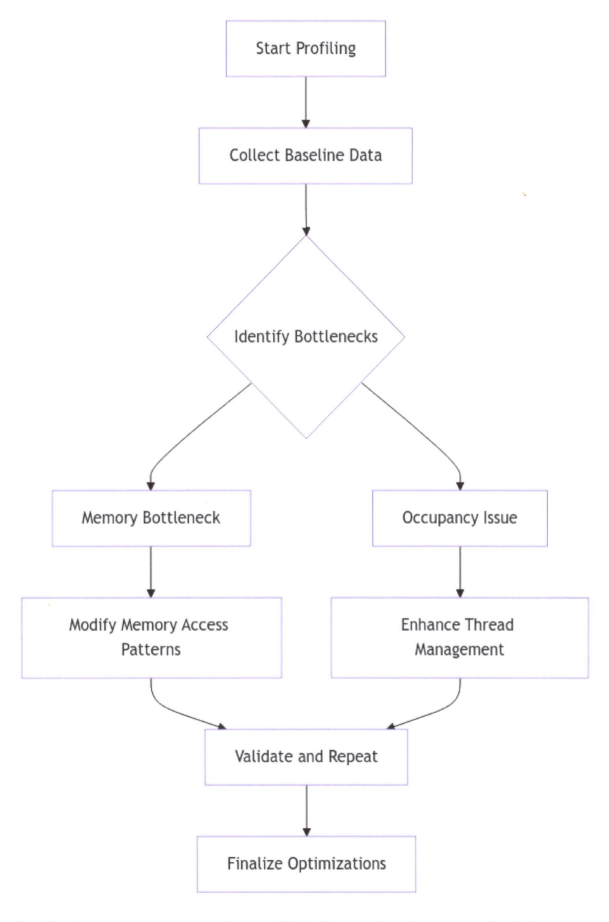

By following a systematic approach using Nsight Compute's tools, you can effectively optimize your CUDA kernels. Be persistent in profiling, analyzing, and iterating on your code to achieve the best possible performance.

Chapter 11: Debugging at Scale with Nsight Systems 2024

In the realm of CUDA programming, achieving optimal performance is paramount, particularly as applications scale. However, identifying performance bottlenecks and understanding application behavior across complex systems can be daunting. This chapter focuses on leveraging Nsight Systems 2024, a comprehensive performance analysis tool tailored for CUDA applications. We will explore how Nsight Systems aids in debugging and performance profiling at scale.

Starting with an overview of Nsight Systems' capabilities, we'll look into setting up an efficient debugging environment. By utilizing its advanced features, including timeline analysis and detailed system-wide profiling, you will learn how to pinpoint inefficiencies and enhance computational throughput. With practical examples and strategic insights, this chapter equips you with the necessary skills to tackle debugging challenges effectively, ensuring your CUDA applications run smoothly and efficiently on modern architectures.

Chapter 11: Debugging CUDA Applications Across Multiple Nodes with Nsight Systems

Debugging CUDA applications, especially when they run across multiple nodes, can be a challenging task. Nsight Systems 2024 provides comprehensive tools and techniques for identifying and solving performance bottlenecks in distributed CUDA applications. Here, we will explore best practices and methodologies for effectively debugging these complex scenarios.

Understanding the Debugging Landscape

When debugging CUDA applications across multiple nodes, it is crucial to have a clear understanding of how data and tasks are distributed. Nsight Systems provides a powerful visualization of the interaction between CPU and GPU threads, the communication between nodes, and the allocation of tasks. This visibility allows for pinpointing issues related to synchronization, data transfer inefficiencies, and workload imbalances.

Setting Up Nsight Systems

To effectively debug applications with Nsight Systems, start by ensuring your environment is correctly configured. This involves:

1. **Installing Nsight Systems**: Make sure you have the latest version compatible with your CUDA release.
2. **Configuring MPI**: If your application uses MPI for inter-node communication, ensure it is correctly set up.

Best Practices in Debugging

1. Modular Code Design

Design your application in a modular way to simplify debugging. Each module should handle distinct functionality, making it easier to isolate issues.

```
#include <iostream>
#include <mpi.h>

```

```
4   void computeOnGPU();
5   void transferData();
6   void processResults();
7
8   int main(int argc, char** argv) {
9       MPI_Init(&argc, &argv);
10
11      computeOnGPU();        // Modular function for GPU computation
12      transferData();        // Modular function for data transfer
13      processResults();      // Modular function for processing results
14
15      MPI_Finalize();
16      return 0;
17  }
18
19  // Implementation of computeOnGPU, transferData, and processResults
```

2. Use of Asynchronous Operations

Leverage CUDA streams and non-blocking MPI operations to maximize overlap of computation and communication.

```
1   #include <cuda_runtime.h>
2   #include <mpi.h>
3
4   // Kernel to perform GPU computation
5   __global__ void gpuKernel() {
6       // Simple kernel for illustration
7   }
8
9   void computeOnGPU() {
10      cudaStream_t stream;
11      cudaStreamCreate(&stream);
12
13      gpuKernel<<<1, 256, 0, stream>>>();
14      cudaStreamSynchronize(stream);
15
16      cudaStreamDestroy(stream);
17  }
```

3. Profiling with Nsight Systems

Profile your application to identify bottlenecks: - **Capture GPU Activities**: Understand the GPU workload distribution. - **Track MPI Usage**: Ensure there are no unexpected delays in inter-node communication.

```
1   nsys profile --trace=cuda,mpi ./your_cuda_app
```

Analyze the profiling report to visualize the execution timeline and identify areas to optimize.

Visualizing Processes

Use visual representations to better understand the flow of data and tasks.

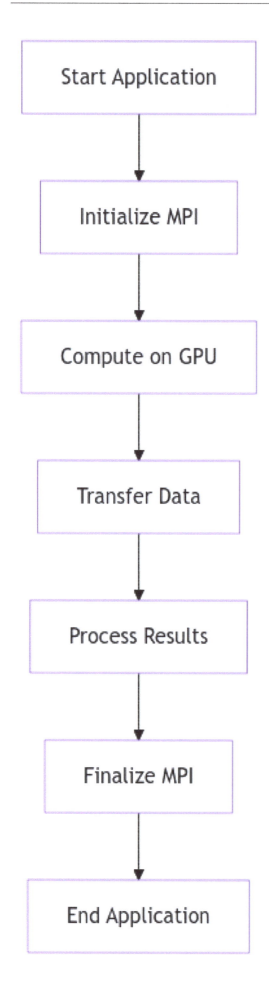

Conclusion

Debugging CUDA applications across multiple nodes is manageable with the right tools and strategies. By adopting modular designs, leveraging asynchronous operations, and utilizing Nsight Systems for profiling, you can effectively diagnose and optimize your distributed applications. Remember to iteratively profile, analyze, and refine your application for improved performance and efficiency.

11.2 Identifying Performance Bottlenecks in Multi-GPU Environments

In modern CUDA programming, utilizing multiple GPUs can significantly enhance computational performance. However, achieving optimal performance across a multi-GPU setup requires careful identification and resolution of performance bottlenecks. Nsight Systems 2024 provides a comprehensive toolkit to debug and optimize multi-GPU applications. This section explores methodologies for identifying potential bottlenecks using Nsight Systems, combined with clean, modular C++ code.

Common Bottlenecks in Multi-GPU Applications

1. **Data Transfer Overheads**: Excessive data transfer between host and GPUs can curtail performance. Minimizing such transfers or using asynchronous operations can mitigate this bottleneck.

2. **Kernel Launch Overhead**: Frequent kernel launches can cause significant delays. Combining operations into fewer kernels or using stream-based parallelism can reduce overhead.

3. **Load Imbalance**: Uneven workload distribution across GPUs leads to suboptimal performance. Use workload balancing strategies to ensure even distribution.

4. **Synchronization Issues**: Excessive synchronization between GPUs can slow down execution. Reducing unnecessary synchronization and optimizing necessary ones is key.

Utilizing Nsight Systems

Nsight Systems 2024 provides an in-depth analysis of GPU usage, highlighting bottlenecks. Follow these steps to identify and analyze bottlenecks:

- **Profile the Application**: Start by profiling your application thoroughly. Nsight Systems provides timelines that show GPU utilization, data transfers, kernel launches, and more.

- **Analyze Timelines**: Look for gaps or underutilized periods in GPU timelines, indicating potential bottlenecks.

- **Check for H2D and D2H Transfers**: Identify excessive host-to-device (H2D) and device-to-host (D2H) transfers.

- **Monitor Kernel Execution**: Review kernel execution times and identify any with significantly longer durations.

C++ Code Example

By adhering to DRY and KISS principles, the following C++ example demonstrates a modular approach to manage multi-GPU execution efficiently:

```cpp
#include <iostream>
#include <vector>
#include <cuda_runtime.h>

#define N 1024
#define CHECK_CUDA(call)                                                    \
    {                                                                       \
        cudaError_t err = call;                                             \
        if (err != cudaSuccess) {                                           \
            std::cerr << "CUDA error in " << __FILE__ << " at line " <<     \
                __LINE__ << ": " \
                    << cudaGetErrorString(err) << std::endl;                \
            exit(1);                                                        \
        }                                                                   \
    }

// Simple kernel to add vectors
__global__ void vectorAdd(const float* A, const float* B, float* C, int
    numElements) {
    int i = blockDim.x * blockIdx.x + threadIdx.x;
    if (i < numElements) {
        C[i] = A[i] + B[i];
    }
}

// Initialize vector data
void initializeData(std::vector<float>& vec) {
    for (auto& val : vec) {
        val = static_cast<float>(rand()) / RAND_MAX;
    }
}

// Launch kernel for a specific GPU
void launchKernelOnGPU(int gpuId, const float* d_A, const float* d_B, float
    * d_C, int numElements) {
    CHECK_CUDA(cudaSetDevice(gpuId));
    int threadsPerBlock = 256;
    int blocksPerGrid = (numElements + threadsPerBlock - 1) /
        threadsPerBlock;
    vectorAdd<<<blocksPerGrid, threadsPerBlock>>>(d_A, d_B, d_C,
        numElements);
    CHECK_CUDA(cudaDeviceSynchronize());
}

int main() {
    int numGPUs;
    CHECK_CUDA(cudaGetDeviceCount(&numGPUs));
```

```cpp
    if (numGPUs < 2) {
        std::cerr << "This example requires at least 2 GPUs." << std::endl;
        return -1;
    }

    std::vector<float> h_A(N), h_B(N), h_C(N);
    initializeData(h_A);
    initializeData(h_B);

    std::vector<float*> d_A(numGPUs), d_B(numGPUs), d_C(numGPUs);
    for (int i = 0; i < numGPUs; ++i) {
        CHECK_CUDA(cudaSetDevice(i));
        CHECK_CUDA(cudaMalloc((void**)&d_A[i], N * sizeof(float)));
        CHECK_CUDA(cudaMalloc((void**)&d_B[i], N * sizeof(float)));
        CHECK_CUDA(cudaMalloc((void**)&d_C[i], N * sizeof(float)));

        CHECK_CUDA(cudaMemcpy(d_A[i], h_A.data(), N * sizeof(float),
            cudaMemcpyHostToDevice));
        CHECK_CUDA(cudaMemcpy(d_B[i], h_B.data(), N * sizeof(float),
            cudaMemcpyHostToDevice));
    }

    for (int i = 0; i < numGPUs; ++i) {
        launchKernelOnGPU(i, d_A[i], d_B[i], d_C[i], N);
    }

    for (int i = 0; i < numGPUs; ++i) {
        CHECK_CUDA(cudaMemcpy(h_C.data(), d_C[i], N * sizeof(float),
            cudaMemcpyDeviceToHost));
        std::cout << "GPU " << i << " completed processing." << std::endl;
    }

    for (int i = 0; i < numGPUs; ++i) {
        CHECK_CUDA(cudaFree(d_A[i]));
        CHECK_CUDA(cudaFree(d_B[i]));
        CHECK_CUDA(cudaFree(d_C[i]));
    }

    return 0;
}
```

Conclusion

Efficient multi-GPU programming requires a strategic approach to minimize bottlenecks. Using tools like Nsight Systems 2024, developers can gain insights into their applications, allowing them to optimize performance effectively. By implementing best practices, such as reducing data transfer overhead and ensuring load balance, you can substantially improve your multi-GPU application's performance.

Chapter 11: Profiling Memory and GPU Utilization with the Latest NVML Tools

Profiling is an essential step in optimizing CUDA applications to ensure efficient usage of memory and GPU resources. NVML (NVIDIA Management Library) provides tools for monitoring and managing various states and resources of NVIDIA GPUs, making it invaluable for performance tuning and debugging at scale.

NVML Overview

NVML is designed to allow developers to query GPU usage, memory statistics, and other valuable metrics directly from their applications. NVML allows for seamless integration into your existing C++ codebase, provided you adhere to best practices like DRY and KISS, and ensure modularity.

NVML Setup

Before using NVML, you must ensure that it is correctly installed and included in your project. You can link the NVML library by including the header and linking against the shared library:

```
#include <nvml.h>
```

To initialize NVML, use the following function call:

```
nvmlReturn_t result = nvmlInit();
if (NVML_SUCCESS != result) {
    std::cerr << "Failed to initialize NVML: " << nvmlErrorString(result)
        << std::endl;
    exit(1);
}
```

Profiling Memory Usage

To profile memory utilization, you can query the free and total memory on a GPU using NVML. This information can help in determining memory bottlenecks or inefficiencies in your CUDA application.

```
nvmlDevice_t device;
nvmlMemory_t memoryInfo;

// Assume the first GPU is the target device
result = nvmlDeviceGetHandleByIndex(0, &device);
if (NVML_SUCCESS != result) {
    std::cerr << "Failed to get handle for device 0: " << nvmlErrorString(
        result) << std::endl;
    exit(1);
}

// Query memory information
result = nvmlDeviceGetMemoryInfo(device, &memoryInfo);
if (NVML_SUCCESS != result) {
    std::cerr << "Failed to get memory info: " << nvmlErrorString(result)
        << std::endl;
} else {
    std::cout << "Total memory: " << memoryInfo.total / (1024 * 1024) << "
        MB\n";
    std::cout << "Used memory: " << memoryInfo.used / (1024 * 1024) << " MB
        \n";
    std::cout << "Free memory: " << memoryInfo.free / (1024 * 1024) << " MB
        \n";
}
```

Profiling GPU Utilization

To monitor the GPU utilization, NVML provides a straightforward method to check the GPU's current load:

```cpp
unsigned int utilization;
result = nvmlDeviceGetUtilizationRates(device, &utilization);

if (NVML_SUCCESS != result) {
    std::cerr << "Failed to get utilization rates: " << nvmlErrorString(
        result) << std::endl;
} else {
    std::cout << "GPU utilization: " << utilization.gpu << " %\n";
    std::cout << "Memory utilization: " << utilization.memory << " %\n";
}
```

Cleanup

After profiling, ensure NVML is properly shut down to release resources and prevent memory leaks:

```cpp
result = nvmlShutdown();
if (NVML_SUCCESS != result) {
    std::cerr << "Failed to shutdown NVML: " << nvmlErrorString(result) <<
        std::endl;
}
```

Conclusion

Using NVML for profiling offers a powerful way to obtain insights into the performance of your CUDA applications. By integrating these profiling tools early in the development process, you can identify and address potential performance issues, ensuring your applications run optimally across different scales.

For a visual representation of the relationships in the NVML library and function calls, consider the following diagram:

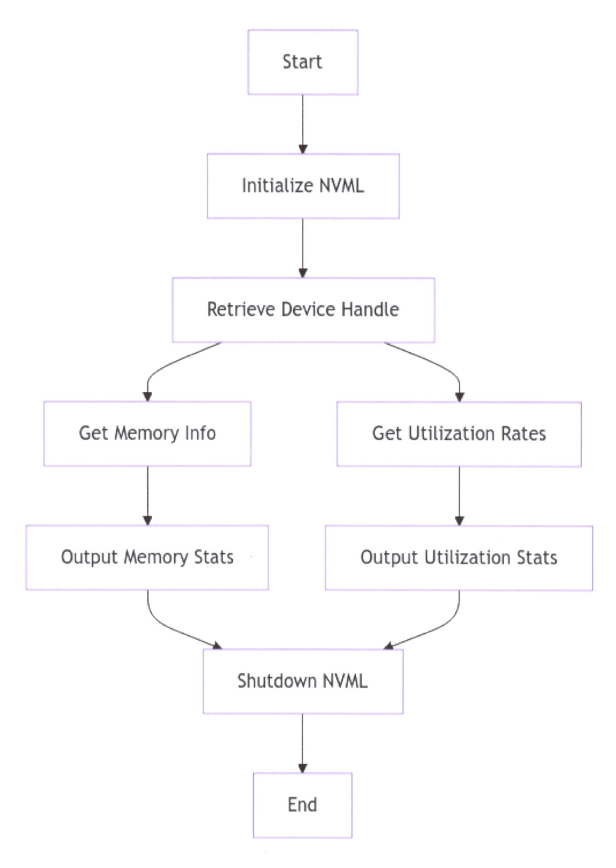

Incorporating NVML into your CUDA projects can significantly enhance your ability to diagnose and troubleshoot performance bottlenecks, paving the way for more efficient and scalable CUDA applications.

Chapter 12: Appendix A: Extended Sample Programs for Numerical Calculations

In this appendix, we explore a suite of extended sample programs designed to demonstrate the practical applications of CUDA programming in numerical calculations. These examples serve to reinforce concepts covered in earlier chapters, illustrating how CUDA can be leveraged to optimize computationally intensive tasks.

We'll begin by examining foundational numerical algorithms, providing insight into the parallelization of these methods. Each sample program is crafted to highlight modular code design and the effective use of CUDA's parallel architecture, ensuring clarity and reusability.

The appendix covers:

- Matrix operations, showcasing optimizations for large datasets.
- Parallel reduction techniques for efficient data aggregation.
- The implementation of numerical integration methods to demonstrate CUDA's ability to handle continuous calculations.
- Examples of solving differential equations, illustrating how CUDA accelerates complex mathematical models.

By providing these examples, the appendix aims to equip readers with the tools needed to tackle advanced numerical problems, bridging theory and practical application in CUDA programming.

12.1 Sample programs for holography, Monte Carlo simulations, FDTD, and heat conduction problems in Fortran, optimised for CUDA 12.6.

Appendix A: Extended Sample Programs for Numerical Calculations

Sample Programs for Holography, Monte Carlo Simulations, FDTD, and Heat Conduction Problems

In this section, we explore sample programs for various scientific computations, optimized for CUDA 12.6. Each example aims to illustrate the implementation of numerical methods using both Fortran and C++, leveraging the power of CUDA for parallel computation. We'll focus on modular, reusable code while adhering to DRY and KISS principles.

Holography

Concept: Holography involves interference and diffraction to record and reconstruct the light field.

Fortran Sample

```fortran
module holography_mod
  implicit none
contains
  subroutine compute_holography(data, hologram)
    real, intent(in) :: data(:)
    real, intent(out) :: hologram(size(data))
    ! Implement holography algorithm
    ! Pseudocode for simplicity
    hologram = data * 2.0  ! Placeholder operation
  end subroutine compute_holography
end module holography_mod
```

C++ CUDA Sample

```cpp
#include <cuda_runtime.h>
#include <vector>

// Kernel function for holography
__global__ void computeHolographyKernel(const float* data, float* hologram,
    int n) {
    int idx = threadIdx.x + blockIdx.x * blockDim.x;
    if (idx < n) {
        hologram[idx] = data[idx] * 2.0f;  // Placeholder operation
    }
}

// Host function
void computeHolography(const std::vector<float>& data, std::vector<float>&
    hologram) {
    int n = data.size();
    float *d_data, *d_hologram;

    // Allocate device memory
    cudaMalloc(&d_data, n * sizeof(float));
    cudaMalloc(&d_hologram, n * sizeof(float));

    // Copy data to device
    cudaMemcpy(d_data, data.data(), n * sizeof(float),
        cudaMemcpyHostToDevice);

    // Launch kernel
    computeHolographyKernel<<<(n + 255) / 256, 256>>>(d_data, d_hologram, n
        );

    // Copy result back to host
    cudaMemcpy(hologram.data(), d_hologram, n * sizeof(float),
        cudaMemcpyDeviceToHost);

    // Free device memory
    cudaFree(d_data);
    cudaFree(d_hologram);
}
```

Monte Carlo Simulations

Concept: Monte Carlo methods use random sampling to solve problems that might be deterministic in nature.

Fortran Sample

```fortran
module monte_carlo_mod
  implicit none
contains
  function estimate_pi(num_samples) result(pi_estimate)
    integer, intent(in) :: num_samples
    real :: pi_estimate
    integer :: i, count
    real :: x, y
    count = 0
    do i = 1, num_samples
      call random_number(x)
```

```fortran
      call random_number(y)
      if (x*x + y*y <= 1.0) count = count + 1
    end do
    pi_estimate = 4.0 * count / num_samples
  end function estimate_pi
end module monte_carlo_mod
```

C++ CUDA Sample

```cpp
#include <curand_kernel.h>

__global__ void monteCarloPiKernel(int* count, int num_samples, unsigned
    long seed) {
    int idx = threadIdx.x + blockIdx.x * blockDim.x;
    curandState state;
    curand_init(seed, idx, 0, &state);

    int local_count = 0;
    for (int i = idx; i < num_samples; i += blockDim.x * gridDim.x) {
        float x = curand_uniform(&state);
        float y = curand_uniform(&state);
        if (x*x + y*y <= 1.0f) ++local_count;
    }

    atomicAdd(count, local_count);
}

float estimatePi(int num_samples) {
    int h_count = 0;
    int* d_count;
    cudaMalloc(&d_count, sizeof(int));
    cudaMemcpy(d_count, &h_count, sizeof(int), cudaMemcpyHostToDevice);

    monteCarloPiKernel<<<(num_samples + 255) / 256, 256>>>(d_count,
        num_samples, time(NULL));
    cudaMemcpy(&h_count, d_count, sizeof(int), cudaMemcpyDeviceToHost);

    cudaFree(d_count);
    return 4.0f * h_count / num_samples;
}
```

Finite-Difference Time-Domain (FDTD)

Concept: FDTD is a numerical analysis technique to model computational electrodynamics by solving Maxwell's equations.

Fortran Sample

```fortran
module fdtd_mod
  implicit none
contains
  subroutine fdtd_step(electric_field, magnetic_field)
    real, intent(inout) :: electric_field(:,:)
    real, intent(inout) :: magnetic_field(:,:)
    ! Placeholder update for fields
    electric_field = electric_field + 0.1
    magnetic_field = magnetic_field + 0.1
```

```
10    end subroutine fdtd_step
11  end module fdtd_mod
```

C++ CUDA Sample

```cpp
1  __global__ void fdtdStepKernel(float* electricField, float* magneticField,
      int width, int height) {
2    int x = threadIdx.x + blockIdx.x * blockDim.x;
3    int y = threadIdx.y + blockIdx.y * blockDim.y;
4    if (x < width && y < height) {
5        int idx = x + y * width;
6        electricField[idx] += 0.1f;   // Placeholder operation
7        magneticField[idx] += 0.1f;   // Placeholder operation
8    }
9  }
10
11  void fdtdStep(std::vector<float>& electricField, std::vector<float>&
      magneticField, int width, int height) {
12    float *d_electricField, *d_magneticField;
13    size_t size = width * height * sizeof(float);
14
15    cudaMalloc(&d_electricField, size);
16    cudaMalloc(&d_magneticField, size);
17
18    cudaMemcpy(d_electricField, electricField.data(), size,
          cudaMemcpyHostToDevice);
19    cudaMemcpy(d_magneticField, magneticField.data(), size,
          cudaMemcpyHostToDevice);
20
21    dim3 threadsPerBlock(16, 16);
22    dim3 blocksPerGrid((width + 15) / 16, (height + 15) / 16);
23    fdtdStepKernel<<<blocksPerGrid, threadsPerBlock>>>(d_electricField,
          d_magneticField, width, height);
24
25    cudaMemcpy(electricField.data(), d_electricField, size,
          cudaMemcpyDeviceToHost);
26    cudaMemcpy(magneticField.data(), d_magneticField, size,
          cudaMemcpyDeviceToHost);
27
28    cudaFree(d_electricField);
29    cudaFree(d_magneticField);
30  }
```

Heat Conduction

Concept: Heat conduction problems are usually modeled by solving heat diffusion equations over a domain.

Fortran Sample

```fortran
1  module heat_conduction_mod
2    implicit none
3  contains
4    subroutine update_temperature(temperature)
5      real, intent(inout) :: temperature(:,:)
6      ! Simple diffusion step
7      temperature = temperature + 0.1
```

```
8    end subroutine update_temperature
9  end module heat_conduction_mod
```

C++ CUDA Sample

```
1  __global__ void heatConductionKernel(float* temperature, int width, int
     height) {
2      int x = threadIdx.x + blockIdx.x * blockDim.x;
3      int y = threadIdx.y + blockIdx.y * blockDim.y;
4      if (x < width && y < height) {
5          int idx = x + y * width;
6          temperature[idx] += 0.1f;   // Placeholder operation
7      }
8  }
9
10 void updateTemperature(std::vector<float>& temperature, int width, int
      height) {
11     float* d_temperature;
12     size_t size = width * height * sizeof(float);
13
14     cudaMalloc(&d_temperature, size);
15     cudaMemcpy(d_temperature, temperature.data(), size,
          cudaMemcpyHostToDevice);
16
17     dim3 threadsPerBlock(16, 16);
18     dim3 blocksPerGrid((width + 15) / 16, (height + 15) / 16);
19     heatConductionKernel<<<blocksPerGrid, threadsPerBlock>>>(d_temperature,
          width, height);
20
21     cudaMemcpy(temperature.data(), d_temperature, size,
          cudaMemcpyDeviceToHost);
22     cudaFree(d_temperature);
23 }
```

Each of these programs demonstrates a basic structure for problem-solving with CUDA, focusing on clean and efficient code. By modularizing code into kernels and functions, we ensure that these solutions remain both simple and effective for a range of input sizes and configurations.

Chapter 13: Appendix B: Further Reading

This appendix is designed to be an invaluable resource for both novice and experienced CUDA programmers. As you progress through your journey of mastering CUDA, staying informed about the latest advancements, tools, and best practices is crucial. While this book provides a comprehensive foundation, continual learning from additional resources will enhance your understanding and proficiency.

In this section, you'll discover a carefully curated list of books, research papers, articles, and online resources that look deeper into various aspects of CUDA programming. Whether you're looking for detailed explanations of advanced topics, seeking optimization techniques, or exploring real-world applications, these resources will serve as your guide to expanding your knowledge beyond the scope of this book.

By engaging with these materials, you'll not only keep your skills up-to-date but also gain new insights and perspectives that can be applied to your CUDA projects.

13.1 Recommended Books, Articles, and Resources

In the realm of CUDA programming, continual learning is key to mastering the complexities of GPU computing. Below is a curated list of books, articles, and resources that cover everything from the basics to advanced techniques in CUDA programming.

Books

1. **"Programming Massively Parallel Processors: A Hands-on Approach" by David B. Kirk and Wen-mei W. Hwu**
   - This book is a comprehensive guide to understanding parallel programming and CUDA architecture. It provides practical examples and case studies that illustrate GPU computing applications.
2. **"CUDA by Example: An Introduction to General-Purpose GPU Programming" by Jason Sanders and Edward Kandrot**
   - Designed for beginners, this book offers a step-by-step introduction to CUDA. The examples are simple yet effective, demonstrating how to leverage GPU capabilities.
3. **"CUDA for Engineers: An Introduction to High-Performance Parallel Computing" by Duane Storti and Mete Yurtoglu**
   - Aimed at engineers and scientists, this book integrates CUDA programming with real-world applications, emphasizing computational thinking and problem-solving.

Articles

1. **"An Introduction to CUDA" by Mark Harris**
   - This article provides a beginner-friendly introduction to CUDA, covering fundamental concepts like threads, blocks, and the execution model. It's available on the NVIDIA Developer Blog.
2. **"Optimizing CUDA Applications" by Stephen Jones**
   - Published by NVIDIA, this article looks into optimization strategies for CUDA applications, helping developers enhance performance and efficiency.

Online Courses

1. **NVIDIA's "CUDA Training and Courses"**
   - NVIDIA offers a range of online courses that cater to different skill levels. These courses are designed by experts and provide hands-on experience with CUDA programming.
2. **Coursera's "Introduction to Parallel Programming" by UC Davis**
   - This course covers the basics of parallel computing with a focus on CUDA. It includes interactive programming assignments to reinforce learning.

Code Examples and Best Practices

Here's a simple example illustrating the principles of memory management in CUDA, focusing on best practices:

```
#include <iostream>
#include <cuda_runtime.h>

// Kernel to add elements of two arrays
__global__ void addArrays(const int* a, const int* b, int* c, int size) {
    int idx = threadIdx.x + blockIdx.x * blockDim.x;
    if (idx < size) {
        c[idx] = a[idx] + b[idx];
```

```cpp
     }
}

// Utility function to handle CUDA errors
void cudaCheckError(cudaError_t err, const char* msg) {
    if (err != cudaSuccess) {
        std::cerr << "Error: " << msg << ": " << cudaGetErrorString(err) <<
            '\n';
        exit(EXIT_FAILURE);
    }
}

// Host function to allocate and manage memory
void addArraysHost(const int* a, const int* b, int* c, int size) {
    int *d_a, *d_b, *d_c;
    size_t bytes = size * sizeof(int);

    // Allocate device memory
    cudaCheckError(cudaMalloc((void**)&d_a, bytes), "Failed to allocate
        device memory for a");
    cudaCheckError(cudaMalloc((void**)&d_b, bytes), "Failed to allocate
        device memory for b");
    cudaCheckError(cudaMalloc((void**)&d_c, bytes), "Failed to allocate
        device memory for c");

    // Copy data from host to device
    cudaCheckError(cudaMemcpy(d_a, a, bytes, cudaMemcpyHostToDevice), "
        Failed to copy data from a to d_a");
    cudaCheckError(cudaMemcpy(d_b, b, bytes, cudaMemcpyHostToDevice), "
        Failed to copy data from b to d_b");

    // Launch kernel
    int blockSize = 256;
    int gridSize = (size + blockSize - 1) / blockSize;
    addArrays<<<gridSize, blockSize>>>(d_a, d_b, d_c, size);

    // Check for kernel errors
    cudaCheckError(cudaGetLastError(), "Kernel launch failed");

    // Copy result back to host
    cudaCheckError(cudaMemcpy(c, d_c, bytes, cudaMemcpyDeviceToHost), "
        Failed to copy data from d_c to c");

    // Free device memory
    cudaFree(d_a);
    cudaFree(d_b);
    cudaFree(d_c);
}

int main() {
    const int size = 1000;
    int a[size], b[size], c[size];

    // Initialize arrays
    for (int i = 0; i < size; ++i) {
        a[i] = i;
        b[i] = i * 2;
    }
```

```
60
61     // Perform addition
62     addArraysHost(a, b, c, size);
63
64     // Verify results
65     for (int i = 0; i < size; ++i) {
66         if (c[i] != a[i] + b[i]) {
67             std::cerr << "Error at index " << i << ": " << c[i] << " != "
                   << a[i] + b[i] << '\n';
68             return EXIT_FAILURE;
69         }
70     }
71
72     std::cout << "All values computed correctly.\n";
73     return EXIT_SUCCESS;
74 }
```

Visualization

Below is a visualization of CUDA's execution model to illustrate how threads, blocks, and the grid interact.

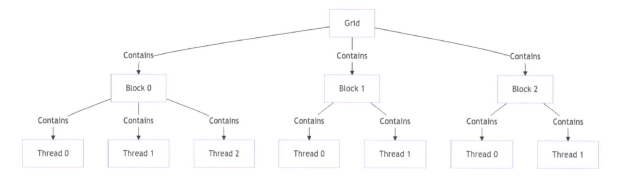

These resources provide a solid foundation for anyone looking to deepen their understanding of CUDA programming, from academics to practitioners in the field.